IELTS
GENERAL TRAINING 19

WITH ANSWERS

AUTHENTIC PRACTICE TESTS

 WITH AUDIO

Shaftesbury Road, Cambridge CB2 8EA, United Kingdom

One Liberty Plaza, 20th Floor, New York, NY 10006, USA

477 Williamstown Road, Port Melbourne, VIC 3207, Australia

314–321, 3rd Floor, Plot 3, Splendor Forum, Jasola District Centre, New Delhi – 110025, India

103 Penang Road, #05–06/07, Visioncrest Commercial, Singapore 238467

Cambridge University Press & Assessment is a department of the University of Cambridge.

We share the University's mission to contribute to society through the pursuit of education, learning and research at the highest international levels of excellence.

www.cambridge.org
Information on this title: www.cambridge.org/9781009454742

© Cambridge University Press & Assessment 2024

This publication is in copyright. Subject to statutory exception and to the provisions of relevant collective licensing agreements, no reproduction of any part may take place without the written permission of Cambridge University Press & Assessment.

First published 2024

20 19 18 17 16 15 14 13 12 11 10 9 8 7 6 5 4 3 2 1

Printed in Dubai by Oriental Press

A catalogue record for this publication is available from the British Library

ISBN 978-1-009-45474-2 General Training Student's Book with Answers with Audio with Resource Bank

Cambridge University Press & Assessment has no responsibility for the persistence or accuracy of URLs for external or third-party internet websites referred to in this publication and does not guarantee that any content on such websites is, or will remain, accurate or appropriate. Information regarding prices, travel timetables, and other factual information given in this work is correct at the time of first printing but Cambridge University Press & Assessment does not guarantee the accuracy of such information thereafter.

Contents

Introduction 4

Test 1 10

Test 2 32

Test 3 55

Test 4 77

Audioscripts 100

Listening and Reading answer keys 121

Sample Writing answers 129

Sample answer sheets 141

Introduction

Prepare for the exam with practice tests from Cambridge

Inside you'll find four authentic examination papers from Cambridge University Press & Assessment. They are the perfect way to practise – EXACTLY like the real test.

Why are they unique?

All our authentic practice tests go through the same design process as the IELTS test. We check every single part of our practice tests with real students under exam conditions, to make sure we give you the most authentic experience possible.

Students can take these tests on their own or with the help of a teacher to familiarise themselves with the exam format, understand the scoring system and practise exam technique.

Further information

IELTS is jointly managed by the British Council, IDP: IELTS Australia and Cambridge University Press & Assessment. Further information can be found on the IELTS official website at ielts.org.

WHAT IS THE TEST FORMAT?

IELTS consists of four components. All candidates take the same Listening and Speaking tests. There is a choice of Reading and Writing tests according to whether a candidate is taking the Academic or General Training module.

Academic	General Training
For candidates wishing to study at undergraduate or postgraduate levels, and for those seeking professional registration.	For candidates wishing to migrate to an English-speaking country (Australia, Canada, New Zealand, UK), and for those wishing to train or study below degree level.

Introduction

The test components are taken in the following order:

	Listening 4 parts, 40 items, approximately 30 minutes	
Academic Reading 3 sections, 40 items 60 minutes	or	**General Training Reading** 3 sections, 40 items 60 minutes
Academic Writing 2 tasks 60 minutes	or	**General Training Writing** 2 tasks 60 minutes
	Speaking 11 to 14 minutes	
	Total (Maximum) Test Time 2 hours 44 minutes	

GENERAL TRAINING TEST FORMAT

Listening

This test consists of four parts, each with ten questions. The first two parts are concerned with social needs. The first part is a conversation between two speakers and the second part is a monologue. The final two parts are concerned with situations related to educational or training contexts. The third part is a conversation between up to four people and the fourth part is a monologue.

A variety of question types is used, including: multiple choice, matching, plan/map/diagram labelling, form completion, note completion, table completion, flowchart completion, summary completion, sentence completion and short-answer questions.

Candidates hear the recording once only and answer the questions as they listen. Ten minutes are allowed at the end for candidates to transfer their answers to the answer sheet.

Reading

This test consists of three sections with 40 questions. The texts are taken from notices, advertisements, leaflets, newspapers, instruction manuals, books and magazines. The first section contains texts relevant to basic linguistic survival in English, with tasks mainly concerned with providing factual information. The second section focuses on the work context and involves texts containing more complex language. The third section involves reading more extended texts, with a more complex structure, but with the emphasis on descriptive and instructive rather than argumentative texts.

A variety of question types is used, including: multiple choice, identifying information (True/False/Not Given), identifying the writer's views/claims (Yes/No/Not Given), matching information, matching headings, matching features, matching sentence endings, sentence

Introduction

completion, summary completion, note completion, table completion, flowchart completion, diagram-label completion and short-answer questions.

Writing

This test consists of two tasks. It is suggested that candidates spend about 20 minutes on Task 1, which requires them to write at least 150 words, and 40 minutes on Task 2, which requires them to write at least 250 words. Task 2 contributes twice as much as Task 1 to the Writing score.

In Task 1, candidates are asked to respond to a given situation with a letter requesting information or explaining the situation. They are assessed on their ability to engage in personal correspondence, elicit and provide general factual information, express needs, wants, likes and dislikes, express opinions, complaints, etc.

In Task 2, candidates are presented with a point of view, argument or problem. They are assessed on their ability to provide general factual information, outline a problem and present a solution, present and justify an opinion, and evaluate and challenge ideas, evidence or arguments.

Candidates are also assessed on their ability to write in an appropriate style. More information on assessing the Writing test, including Writing assessment criteria (public version), is available at ielts.org.

Speaking

This test takes between 11 and 14 minutes and is conducted by a trained examiner. There are three parts:

Part 1

The candidate and the examiner introduce themselves. Candidates then answer general questions about themselves, their home/family, their job/studies, their interests and a wide range of similar familiar topic areas. This part lasts between four and five minutes.

Part 2

The candidate is given a task card with prompts and is asked to talk on a particular topic. The candidate has one minute to prepare and they can make some notes if they wish, before speaking for between one and two minutes. The examiner then asks one or two questions on the same topic.

Part 3

The examiner and the candidate engage in a discussion of more abstract issues which are thematically linked to the topic in Part 2. The discussion lasts between four and five minutes.

The Speaking test assesses whether candidates can communicate effectively in English. The assessment takes into account Fluency and Coherence, Lexical Resource, Grammatical Range and Accuracy, and Pronunciation. More information on assessing the Speaking test, including Speaking assessment criteria (public version), is available at ielts.org.

Introduction

HOW IS IELTS SCORED?

IELTS results are reported on a nine-band scale. In addition to the score for overall language ability, IELTS provides a score in the form of a profile for each of the four skills (Listening, Reading, Writing and Speaking). These scores are also reported on a nine-band scale. All scores are recorded on the Test Report Form along with details of the candidate's nationality, first language and date of birth. Each Overall Band Score corresponds to a descriptive statement which gives a summary of the English-language ability of a candidate classified at that level. The nine bands and their descriptive statements are as follows:

9   **Expert user** – Has fully operational command of the language: appropriate, accurate and fluent with complete understanding.

8   **Very good user** – Has fully operational command of the language with only occasional unsystematic inaccuracies and inappropriacies. Misunderstandings may occur in unfamiliar situations. Handles complex detailed argumentation well.

7   **Good user** – Has operational command of the language, though with occasional inaccuracies, inappropriacies and misunderstandings in some situations. Generally handles complex language well and understands detailed reasoning.

6   **Competent user** – Has generally effective command of the language despite some inaccuracies, inappropriacies and misunderstandings. Can use and understand fairly complex language, particularly in familiar situations.

5   **Modest user** – Has partial command of the language, coping with overall meaning in most situations, though is likely to make many mistakes. Should be able to handle basic communication in own field.

4   **Limited user** – Basic competence is limited to familiar situations. Has frequent problems in understanding and expression. Is not able to use complex language.

3   **Extremely limited user** – Conveys and understands only general meaning in very familiar situations. Frequent breakdowns in communication occur.

2   **Intermittent user** – Has great difficulty understanding spoken and written English.

1   **Non-user** – Essentially has no ability to use the language beyond possibly a few isolated words.

0   **Did not attempt the test** – Did not answer the questions.

Introduction

MARKING THE PRACTICE TESTS

Listening and Reading

The answer keys are on pages 121–128.
Each question in the Listening and Reading tests is worth one mark.

Questions which require letter / Roman numeral answers

For questions where the answers are letters or Roman numerals, you should write *only* the number of answers required. For example, if the answer is a single letter or numeral, you should write only one answer. If you have written more letters or numerals than are required, the answer must be marked wrong.

Questions which require answers in the form of words or numbers

- Answers may be written in upper or lower case.
- Words in brackets are *optional* – they are correct, but not necessary.
- Alternative answers are separated by a slash (/).
- If you are asked to write an answer using a certain number of words and/or (a) number(s), you will be penalised if you exceed this. For example, if a question specifies an answer using NO MORE THAN THREE WORDS and the correct answer is 'black leather coat', the answer 'coat of black leather' is *incorrect*.
- In questions where you are expected to complete a gap, you should only transfer the necessary missing word(s) onto the answer sheet. For example, to complete 'in the . . . ,' where the correct answer is 'morning', the answer 'in the morning' would be *incorrect*.
- All answers require correct spelling (including words in brackets).
- Both US and UK spelling are acceptable and are included in the answer key.
- All standard alternatives for numbers, dates and currencies are acceptable.
- All standard abbreviations are acceptable.
- You will find additional notes about individual answers in the answer key.

Writing

The sample answers are on pages 129–140. It is not possible for you to give yourself a mark for the Writing tasks. We have provided commentaries written by examiners. Additional sample and model answers can be downloaded from the Resource Bank. These sample and model answers will give you an insight into what is required for the Writing test.

HOW SHOULD YOU INTERPRET YOUR SCORES?

At the end of each Listening and Reading answer key you will find a chart which will help you assess whether, on the basis of your practice test results, you are ready to take the IELTS test.

In interpreting your score, there are a number of points you should bear in mind. Your performance in the real IELTS test will be reported in two ways: there will be a Band Score from 1 to 9 for each of the components and an Overall Band Score from 1 to 9, which is the average of your scores in the four components. However, institutions considering your application are advised to look at both the Overall Band Score and the Band Score for each component in order to determine whether you have the language skills needed for a particular course of study or work environment. For example, if you are applying for a course which involves a lot of reading and writing, but no lectures, listening skills might be less important and a score of 5 in Listening might be acceptable if the Overall Band Score was 7. However, for a course which has lots of lectures and spoken instructions, a score of 5 in Listening might be unacceptable even though the Overall Band Score was 7.

Once you have marked your tests, you should have some idea of whether your listening and reading skills are good enough for you to try the IELTS test. If you did well enough in one component, but not in others, you will have to decide for yourself whether you are ready to take the test.

The practice tests have been checked to ensure that they are the same level of difficulty as the real IELTS test. However, we cannot guarantee that your score in the practice tests will be reflected in the real IELTS test. The practice tests can only give you an idea of your possible future performance and it is ultimately up to you to make decisions based on your score.

Different institutions accept different IELTS scores for different types of courses. We have based our recommendations on the average scores which the majority of institutions accept. The institution to which you are applying may, of course, require a higher or lower score than most other institutions.

Test 1

LISTENING

PART 1 **Questions 1–10**

Complete the notes below.

Write **ONE WORD AND/OR A NUMBER** for each answer.

Hinchingbrooke Country Park

The park
Area: **1** .... hectares
Habitats: wetland, grassland and woodland
Wetland: lakes, ponds and a **2** ....
Wildlife includes birds, insects and animals

Subjects studied in educational visits include
Science: children look at **3** .... about plants, etc.
Geography: includes learning to use a **4** .... and compass
History: changes in land use
Leisure and tourism: mostly concentrates on the park's **5** ....
Music: Children make **6** .... with natural materials, and experiment with rhythm and speed.

Benefits of outdoor educational visits
They give children a feeling of **7** .... that they may not have elsewhere.
Children learn new **8** .... and gain self-confidence.

Practical issues
Cost per child: **9** £ ....
Adults, such as **10** .... , free

PART 2 Questions 11–20

Questions 11–15

*Choose the correct letter, **A**, **B** or **C**.*

Stanthorpe Twinning Association

11 During the visit to Malatte, in France, members especially enjoyed

    A   going to a theme park.
    B   experiencing a river trip.
    C   visiting a cheese factory.

12 What will happen in Stanthorpe to mark the 25th anniversary of the Twinning Association?

    A   A tree will be planted.
    B   A garden seat will be bought.
    C   A footbridge will be built.

13 Which event raised most funds this year?

    A   the film show
    B   the pancake evening
    C   the cookery demonstration

14 For the first evening with the French visitors host families are advised to

    A   take them for a walk round the town.
    B   go to a local restaurant.
    C   have a meal at home.

15 On Saturday evening there will be the chance to

    A   listen to a concert.
    B   watch a match.
    C   take part in a competition.

Test 1

Questions 16–20

Label the map below.

Write the correct letter, **A–H**, next to Questions 16–20.

Farley House

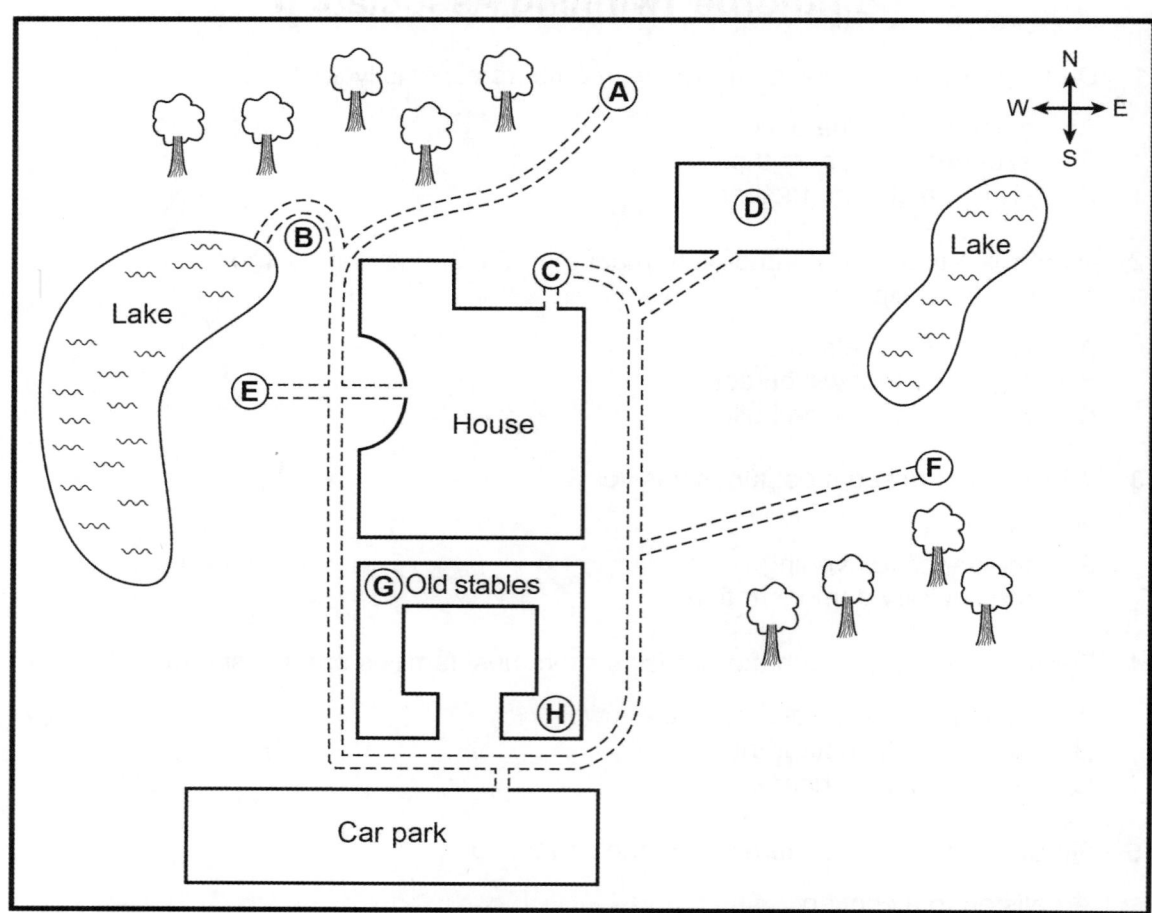

16 Farm shop ....

17 Disabled entry ....

18 Adventure playground ....

19 Kitchen gardens ....

20 The Temple of the Four Winds ....

Listening

PART 3   Questions 21–30

Questions 21 and 22

Choose TWO letters, A–E.

Which **TWO** things did Colin find most satisfying about his bread reuse project?

- A receiving support from local restaurants
- B finding a good way to prevent waste
- C overcoming problems in a basic process
- D experimenting with designs and colours
- E learning how to apply 3-D printing

Questions 23 and 24

Choose TWO letters, A–E.

Which **TWO** ways do the students agree that touch-sensitive sensors for food labels could be developed in future?

- A for use on medical products
- B to show that food is no longer fit to eat
- C for use with drinks as well as foods
- D to provide applications for blind people
- E to indicate the weight of certain foods

Test 1

Questions 25–30

What is the students' opinion about each of the following food trends?

Choose **SIX** answers from the box and write the correct letter, **A–H**, next to Questions 25–30.

Opinions

A   This is only relevant to young people.
B   This may have disappointing results.
C   This already seems to be widespread.
D   Retailers should do more to encourage this.
E   More financial support is needed for this.
F   Most people know little about this.
G   There should be stricter regulations about this.
H   This could be dangerous.

Food trends

25   Use of local products ....
26   Reduction in unnecessary packaging ....
27   Gluten-free and lactose-free food ....
28   Use of branded products related to celebrity chefs ....
29   Development of 'ghost kitchens' for takeaway food ....
30   Use of mushrooms for common health concerns ....

PART 4 Questions 31–40

Complete the notes below.

*Write **ONE WORD ONLY** for each answer.*

Céide Fields

- an important Neolithic archaeological site in the northwest of Ireland

Discovery

- In the 1930s, a local teacher realised that stones beneath the bog surface were once **31** ....
- His **32** .... became an archaeologist and undertook an investigation of the site:
    - a traditional method used by local people to dig for **33** .... was used to identify where stones were located
    - carbon dating later proved the site was Neolithic.
- Items are well preserved in the bog because of a lack of **34** ....

Neolithic farmers

- Houses were **35** .... in shape and had a hole in the roof.
- Neolithic innovations include:
    - cooking indoors
    - pots used for storage and to make **36** ....
- Each field at Céide was large enough to support a big **37** ....
- The fields were probably used to restrict the grazing of animals – no evidence of structures to house them during **38** ....

Reasons for the decline in farming

- a decline in **39** .... quality
- an increase in **40** ....

Test 1

READING

SECTION 1   Questions 1–14

Read the text below and answer Questions 1–7.

Gobridge Tramlink – Frequently Asked Questions (FAQs)

Here are some of the frequently asked questions about the tram service in Gobridge town

When do the trams run?

Gobridge Tramlink operates a network of trams that run throughout the year and provide links to main services, stations and the airport. Timetables are reviewed in October and March, and may alter slightly so check before you travel. Our first tram from the city centre leaves from Marvin Square at 6.30 am, half an hour after the first city bus service.

Can I get a tram from the airport?

Trams from the airport to the city centre start running at 6.15 am and leave every fifteen minutes until 7.30 pm when the evening schedule takes over. Trams then run to the main railway station at 35-minute intervals and end at 11.35 pm. If your flight arrives later than this, the number 207 airport bus runs every hour through the night.

What do I do if I don't have a ticket?

Tickets are not sold by anyone on the tram. Ticket vending machines are located at all tram shelters. Check your route and make sure you buy the correct price ticket. If the vending machine does not work, you should push the red button on the machine and speak into the microphone. A member of staff will either fix the machine straight away or contact the tram inspector onboard your tram. He or she cannot sell you a ticket, but you will not be obliged to pay the £8 on-board fine for not having one.

Can I take my bike on the tram?

Each tram is licensed to carry a maximum of two bicycles, though drivers may refuse to allow cyclists to get on if the tram is crowded. Bicycles may only be taken on the trams during off-peak travel periods: up to 7.30 am, between 10 am and 2.30 pm and after 7 pm. Festivals and other large events may also mean that bicycles are prohibited as trams carry extra passengers at these times. Once on board, riders should remain with their bicycles throughout the journey and ensure they do not obstruct the entrance, exit or any other area of public access.

Reading

Questions 1–7

Do the following statements agree with the information given in the text on page 16?

In boxes 1–7 on your answer sheet, write

> **TRUE** *if the statement agrees with the information*
> **FALSE** *if the statement contradicts the information*
> **NOT GIVEN** *if there is no information on this*

1   The city buses start operating later than the trams.
2   You can get a tram from the airport to the city centre up to midnight.
3   The 207 bus service stops at the main railway station.
4   The cost of a tram ticket varies depending on your journey.
5   Bicycles are allowed on the trams between 7.30 am and 10 am.
6   Additional trams run during the Gobridge festival period.
7   Cyclists may be asked to leave the tram if they block the exit.

Test 1

Read the text below and answer Questions 8–14.

Adorable knitwear

Online customer reviews

A   Mary-Anne

I spent a while thinking about buying this sweater because of the price, but I'm glad I finally did. It's a long sweater but that's good as I'm quite tall. I normally find that the sleeves are too short when I try on a top, but not with this one. I tend to take medium but went for large, which was a wise decision as there is plenty of room for a T-shirt underneath when I wear it with jeans.

B   Davina

These sweaters are an ideal weight for office wear. The purple one is pretty, though I expected a lighter shade from the picture. I wear a US size 12 / UK 16, and the medium is big enough to fit over a shirt with room to spare. It has long sleeves that I love to roll up at the wrist. I'm now trying to resist the temptation to buy it in grey too.

C   Naga

This knitted sweater looks great in the pictures. I ordered the olive green with stripes and, although I wasn't sure it was going to look right on me, I was pleasantly surprised when I put it on. It's very soft and I love the long past-the-wrist sleeves too. I opted for the medium, but it was too tight so I exchanged it.

D   Libby

This is the third of your sweaters that I've bought over the past two years. It's true to size and perfect for the winter months, though I should add that its loose knit means it's best to avoid playing with cats or young dogs when you're wearing it as they could pull threads in the body or sleeves.

E   Laura

I couldn't decide which colour to get so I bought the deep blue and the charcoal grey, with every intention of sending one of them back. That didn't happen, of course! I would say both colours match the online pictures. I bought size small, and the length is perfect for me, despite the unnecessarily long sleeves! These sweaters are lovely to wear with jeans but also stylish enough to wear to work.

Reading

Questions 8–14

*Look at the five online customer reviews of sweaters, **A–E**, on page 18.*

For which review are the following statements true?

*Write the correct letter, **A–E**, in boxes 8–14 on your answer sheet.*

NB *You may use any letter more than once.*

8   The colour of the sweater did not match the website image.
9   The customer took some time to decide on the purchase.
10 The customer initially bought the wrong size.
11 The customer changed her mind about returning a sweater.
12 The customer bought a bigger size than she usually does.
13 The sweater can be worn for smart or casual occasions.
14 The customer was worried that the sweater wouldn't suit her.

SECTION 2   Questions 15–27

Read the text below and answer Questions 15–21.

How to become a great leader

Stepping into a new management role can be unnerving. Here's how to inspire your team:

Set the tone of your leadership style from the outset. Be confident, self-assured and respectful with everyone you meet. Speak as you want to be spoken to, and remember to listen. The first few weeks is when people develop their perceptions of you, so work hard to earn their trust. This will be key to effective change and progress.

Part of a leader's brief is to set bold goals. They could take years to achieve, but they need to be specific enough that everyone in the organisation understands them, buys into them and is willing to work together to achieve them.

Don't do everything yourself. Great leaders surround themselves with talented individuals and they should trust them to make things happen. If things need changing, tell people and involve them in making the changes by participating in the design of a new strategy. If the team is too cautious to embrace change, give them one more chance but be clearer about what you want.

Stamp out the 'them and us' culture. In many organisations, employees feel distant from senior management. The message must be plain: we all work together, but leaders need to work hard to ensure this filters through to everyone in the organisation.

Allow time for innovation. It's important to give staff time to come up with new ideas and solutions that will fix new problems. However, be clear that a decision is expected; set a time limit and stick to it.

It is likely that the formula that makes the business you are managing successful will have been created many years ago – but it's important to remember how the business started. Honour those early pioneers and instil a sense of pride across the organisation.

Leaders need to accept that some risk may be required if the situation calls for it. Playing it safe is never a good business rule, and leaders must make sure their business stays ahead by being prepared to act quickly.

Show you are passionate and enthusiastic. People spend a large part of their lives working for an organisation, and having a leader who is genuinely thrilled about its future is hugely inspiring.

Questions 15–21

Complete the sentences below.

*Choose **ONE WORD ONLY** from the text for each answer.*

Write your answers in boxes 15–21 on your answer sheet.

15 Initially, a leader needs to focus on gaining the .... of the staff.

16 A leader should decide on .... that their staff are happy to fulfil.

17 Leaders should involve their staff in the process of producing a different ....

18 If tricky issues arise, leaders should give staff the space to find .... to them.

19 Leaders need to encourage their staff to feel .... in the past achievements of the company.

20 It is important for leaders to agree to a certain degree of .... when necessary.

21 If leaders find the .... of the company exciting, their staff will be more motivated to work hard.

Read the text below and answer Questions 22–27.

Resigning from a job in a professional manner

When you take the decision to resign and move on to another job, you might really want to dance your way out of the door, or get your own back by criticising your boss to the whole office. But you need to resist these temptations because in future you might find you're working with your ex-line manager or other colleagues in a different company.

Letting your manager know

Show courtesy by telling your boss first. Request a meeting to say that you're leaving, following up soon after with an official letter. Before the meeting with your boss, write a list of ongoing tasks along with status updates and suggestions concerning completion.

Use the meeting to clarify any other points, such as your notice period and leaving date, and how you will inform others (colleagues or external clients, contacts and suppliers). Ask about a reference too; your employer may only supply the most basic type but your line manager might also give you a more personal one. Making sure you get a good one can make subsequent job hunting less stressful.

Preparation

Work out how you can ensure a smooth transition and minimise disruption to your employer. There may be a range of things you can do to hand over professionally, such as completing projects, working out the priorities with your line manager, and leaving clear documentation for the successor in your post concerning processes or software.

Your letter of resignation

Keep your letter short. You don't need to give lots of explanations or justification for why you're leaving. Don't be tempted to address the failings of the company or your boss, either. Instead, thanking your employer for the job and mentioning what you appreciated about it is a graceful touch. Here's an idea of what to include:

- First paragraph – the basics
  Inform the employer that you wish to resign and confirm the agreed final date at work.

- Second paragraph – thank your employer
  Mention any particular career-building projects you worked on or opportunities to develop skills and contribute to the employer's goals and successes. You can also mention your appreciation at being able to work in a great team.

- Third paragraph – handover
  State your willingness to finish existing projects and hand over your work smoothly.

Questions 22–27

Complete the notes below.

Choose **ONE WORD ONLY** from the text for each answer.

Write your answers in boxes 22–27 on your answer sheet.

The best way to resign

Avoid all **22** .... to resign in an angry way. Instead follow this procedure:

Arrange a meeting with the boss to:

- mention any projects which are underway and give ideas for their **23** ....
- discuss how much notice you need to give before you go.
- request information on the type of **24** .... you will receive.

Steps you can take before you leave:

- Work to cause as little **25** .... as possible to the organisation.
- Make sure your successor has adequate guidance on the organisation's systems.

In the resignation letter:

- avoid mentioning any **26** .... in the organisation.
- show appreciation for aspects of the job, e.g., the chance to improve your **27** ....
- indicate your wish to leave everything in good order.

Test 1

SECTION 3   Questions 28–40

Read the text on page 22 and answer Questions 28–40.

Questions 28–32

The text on page 22 has five sections, **A–E**.

Choose the correct heading for each section from the list of headings below.

*Write the correct number, **i–viii**, in boxes 28–32 on your answer sheet.*

List of Headings
- i   Why emojis may have a short life
- ii   Ways in which new emojis are designed and made available
- iii   How words and emojis both fulfil new needs in our society
- iv   How emojis are regarded in different ways by different cultures
- v   The use of emojis in different fields and what this means for us
- vi   The rapid spread of a new way of interacting
- vii   How and where emojis were first invented
- viii   The value of emojis for making feelings clear

28   Section **A**
29   Section **B**
30   Section **C**
31   Section **D**
32   Section **E**

Emojis

A Language always changes, of course. This is one of the few constants about it. But it's arguably changing at a faster rate now than at any previous moment in its history. And emojis – the set of picture characters that people use to punctuate their online correspondence – are at the forefront of this frenzy for change.

As a form of global communication, emojis only began their growth in 2011. Four years later, it was estimated that they were being used by over 90 per cent of the online population. In excess of six billion were being sent every day. Their prevalence in the culture was such that Oxford Dictionaries recently chose one as their word of the year. 'Words of the Year' are those judged to be reflective of the 'ethos, mood, or preoccupations of that particular year'. They're very much of their time. And often, once that time has passed, they fade from people's consciousness almost as quickly as they arose.

There's a good chance, then, that the emoji chosen by Oxford Dictionaries – the 'face with tears of joy' – will also appear to be dated in a few years. But the reasons for this offer a fascinating insight into the way that society is evolving. The little yellow circle with dots for eyes acts as a surprisingly good lens through which to view the history of human communication, and to predict its future.

B There are two main reasons why language changes. One is to do with the way that language mirrors the changes in how we relate to each other. As an expression of identity, language is adapted by different groups and different generations to reflect their own sense of self. It also needs to constantly assimilate fresh concepts as these evolve.

Words are being created for these reasons all the time. But what's interesting about emojis is that they've contributed to this ever-expanding storehouse in a different way. At this point in our history, the gaps in our vocabulary are being filled not simply by new words, but by an absolutely new system of expression.

C The second major reason that language changes is down to technology – specifically, the ways in which the technologies we use have an effect on the process of communication itself. Both hardware and new technologies result in us subtly changing the way we interact with each other and also altering the shape of the language we use.

Emojis have evolved as a solution to the needs of mobile communication. In particular, they compensate for the way that computer-mediated messaging on smartphones can sometimes tend towards the emotionally empty. Whereas face-to-face, or even voice-to-voice, conversations can express emotional closeness through facial expression or tone of voice, this is easy to miss when messages are rendered in a few short words on a small screen. Emojis are a means of restoring this emotional framing to an interaction – punctuating your message with a smile.

D But unlike almost any other type of language system, emojis have something akin to a built-in obsolescence. Just as smartphones and their operating systems have a frequent refresh rate, emojis also get routine enhancements. The emojis you have on your phone now will undergo subtle redesigns over the course of time, and extra characters will be added. Because of this, their usefulness is artificially limited.

In the context of communication systems, this is something that's never previously been the case. Twenty years ago, people might have bought a new landline phone when they were tired of the design of their old phone or if they wanted to get one with whatever latest innovation was going around – an inbuilt answering machine, say. But they didn't have to upgrade the language they were using as well.

Emojis, on the other hand, are a case study of how technology and the human capacity for communication are working together – of how the onward march of technology exists at the intersection of consumerism, innovation and design. Moreover, the fact that they're at the front line of a relentless wave of technologically driven change in communications practices encourages – if not necessitates – a great amount of creativity in the way they're used.

E Finally, there's the way they've become implicated in almost all aspects of modern society, from politics and marketing to art and entertainment. Emojis are the subject of musicals and Hollywood films. They're the inspiration for fashion design, art and architecture. They're a staple in advertising and commerce. Understanding why they've become so popular, and how they work, can not only explain something about the nature of language; it can also help us to understand our relationship with technology, society and ourselves.

Questions 33–37

Complete the summary below.

Choose **ONE WORD ONLY** from the text for each answer.

Write your answers in boxes 33–37 on your answer sheet.

The importance of the 'face with tears of joy'

It is probable that before long, an emoji such as the 'face with tears of joy' will seem **33** .... This is of interest as it tells us about developments in **34** ...., providing an effective way to focus on both the **35** .... and the future of human communication.

Changes in language reflect changes in people's relationships. They reflect the ways in which the **36** .... of groups and generations changes over time, and they allow new **37** .... to be included. However, emojis are interesting as they are a system that expresses these ideas in a completely new way.

Test 1

Questions 38–40

Choose the correct letter, **A**, **B**, **C** or **D**.

Write the correct letter in boxes 38–40 on your answer sheet.

38   What does the writer say about 'Words of the Year'?

      A   They include increasing numbers of emojis.
      B   They are soon forgotten by the public.
      C   They are required to have social significance.
      D   They are invented by the writers of dictionaries.

39   The writer says that the usefulness of emojis is limited because

      A   they are constantly being changed.
      B   they may not be correctly interpreted.
      C   they are difficult for some people to update.
      D   they are linked to specific operating systems.

40   What would be the best subtitle for this text?

      A   Will emojis take over from words one day?
      B   How can emojis be made more meaningful?
      C   Are emojis used too much in our society today?
      D   What do emojis tell us about the world we live in?

WRITING

WRITING TASK 1

You should spend about 20 minutes on this task.

> *You would like to reduce your working hours in order to study part time.*
>
> *Write a letter to your boss. In your letter*
> - *explain why you want to reduce your working hours*
> - *say which hours you would like to work*
> - *describe how your part-time studies would benefit your employer*

Write at least 150 words.

You do **NOT** need to write any addresses.

Begin your letter as follows:

Dear ....,

Test 1

WRITING TASK 2

You should spend about 40 minutes on this task.

Write about the following topic:

> *More and more people nowadays visit well-known places to take photographs of themselves, without looking at the place.*
>
> *Why do you think this is happening?*
>
> *Is it a positive or a negative trend?*

Give reasons for your answer and include any relevant examples from your own knowledge or experience.

Write at least 250 words.

SPEAKING

PART 1

The examiner asks you about yourself, your home, work or studies and other familiar topics.

EXAMPLE

International food

- Can you find food from many different countries where you live? [Why/Why not?]
- How often do you eat typical food from other countries? [Why/Why not?]
- Have you ever tried making food from another country? [Why/Why not?]
- What food from your country would you recommend to people from other countries? [Why?]

PART 2

> **Describe a law that was introduced in your country and that you thought was a very good idea.**
>
> **You should say:**
>   what the law was
>   who introduced it
>   when and why it was introduced
>
> **and explain why you thought this law was such a good idea.**

You will have to talk about the topic for one to two minutes. You have one minute to think about what you are going to say. You can make some notes to help you if you wish.

PART 3

Discussion topics:

School rules

Example questions:
What kinds of rules are common in a school?
How important is it to have rules in a school?
What do you recommend should happen if children break school rules?

Working in the legal profession

Example questions:
Can you suggest why many students decide to study law at university?
What are the key personal qualities needed to be a successful lawyer?
Do you agree that working in the legal profession is very stressful?

Test 2

LISTENING

PART 1   Questions 1–10

Questions 1–6

Complete the form below.

Write **ONE WORD AND/OR A NUMBER** for each answer.

Guitar Group

Coordinator:	Gary **1** ....
Level:	**2** ....
Place:	the **3** ....
	4 .... Street
	First floor, Room T347
Time:	Thursday morning at **5** ....
Recommended website:	'The perfect **6** .... '

Questions 7–10

Complete the table below.

Write **ONE WORD ONLY** for each answer.

\multicolumn{3}{c}{**A typical 45-minute guitar lesson**}
Time	Activity	Notes
5 minutes	tuning guitars	using an app or by **7** ....
10 minutes	strumming chords using our thumbs	keeping time while the teacher is **8** ....
15 minutes	playing songs	often listening to a **9** .... of a song
10 minutes	playing single notes and simple tunes	playing together, then **10** ....
5 minutes	noting things to practise at home	

PART 2   Questions 11–20

Questions 11–16

Choose the correct letter, **A**, **B** or **C**.

Working as a lifeboat volunteer

11 What made David leave London and move to Northsea?

    A   He was eager to develop a hobby.
    B   He wanted to work shorter hours.
    C   He found his job in website design unsatisfying.

12 The Lifeboat Institution in Northsea was built with money provided by

    A   a local organisation.
    B   a local resident.
    C   the local council.

13 In his health assessment, the doctor was concerned about the fact that David

    A   might be colour blind.
    B   was rather short-sighted.
    C   had undergone eye surgery.

14 After arriving at the lifeboat station, they aim to launch the boat within

    A   five minutes.
    B   six to eight minutes.
    C   eight and a half minutes.

15 As a 'helmsman', David has the responsibility of deciding

    A   who will be the members of his crew.
    B   what equipment it will be necessary to take.
    C   if the lifeboat should be launched.

16 As well as going out on the lifeboat, David

    A   gives talks on safety at sea.
    B   helps with fundraising.
    C   recruits new volunteers.

Listening

Questions 17 and 18

*Choose **TWO** letters, **A–E**.*

Which **TWO** things does David say about the lifeboat volunteer training?

- **A** The residential course developed his leadership skills.
- **B** The training in use of ropes and knots was quite brief.
- **C** The training exercises have built up his mental strength.
- **D** The casualty care activities were particularly challenging for him.
- **E** The wave tank activities provided practice in survival techniques.

Questions 19 and 20

*Choose **TWO** letters, **A–E**.*

Which **TWO** things does David find most motivating about the work he does?

- **A** working as part of a team
- **B** experiences when working in winter
- **C** being thanked by those he has helped
- **D** the fact that it keeps him fit
- **E** the chance to develop new equipment

Test 2

PART 3   Questions 21–30

Questions 21–24

Choose the correct letter, A, B or C.

21 At first, Don thought the topic of recycling footwear might be too

    A limited in scope.
    B hard to research.
    C boring for listeners.

22 When discussing trainers, Bella and Don disagree about

    A how popular they are among young people.
    B how suitable they are for school.
    C how quickly they wear out.

23 Bella says that she sometimes recycles shoes because

    A they no longer fit.
    B she no longer likes them.
    C they are no longer in fashion.

24 What did the article say that confused Don?

    A Public consumption of footwear has risen.
    B Less footwear is recycled now than in the past.
    C People dispose of more footwear than they used to.

Questions 25–28

What reasons did the recycling manager give for rejecting footwear, according to the students?

Choose **FOUR** answers from the box and write the correct letter, **A–F**, next to Questions 25–28.

	Reasons
A	one shoe was missing
B	the colour of one shoe had faded
C	one shoe had a hole in it
D	the shoes were brand new
E	the shoes were too dirty
F	the stitching on the shoes was broken

Footwear

25 the high-heeled shoes ....

26 the ankle boots ....

27 the baby shoes ....

28 the trainers ....

Questions 29–30

Choose the correct letter, **A**, **B** or **C**.

29 Why did the project to make 'new' shoes out of old shoes fail?

    A   People believed the 'new' pairs of shoes were unhygienic.
    B   There were not enough good parts to use in the old shoes.
    C   The shoes in the 'new' pairs were not completely alike.

30 Bella and Don agree that they can present their topic

    A   from a new angle.
    B   with relevant images.
    C   in a straightforward way.

PART 4 Questions 31–40

Complete the notes below.

Write **ONE WORD ONLY** for each answer.

Tardigrades

- more than 1,000 species, 0.05–1.2 millimetres long
- also known as water 'bears' (due to how they **31** ....) and 'moss piglets'

Physical appearance

- a **32** .... round body and four pairs of legs
- claws or **33** .... for gripping
- absence of respiratory organs
- body filled with a liquid that carries both **34** .... and blood
- mouth shaped like a **35** .... with teeth called stylets

Habitat

- often found at the bottom of a lake or on plants
- very resilient and can exist in very low or high **36** ....

Cryptobiosis

- In dry conditions, they roll into a ball called a 'tun'.
- They stay alive with a much lower metabolism than usual.
- A type of **37** .... ensures their DNA is not damaged.
- Research is underway to find out how many days they can stay alive in **38** ....

Feeding

- consume liquids, e.g., those found in moss or **39** ....
- may eat other tardigrades

Conservation status

- They are not considered to be **40** ....

READING

SECTION 1 Questions 1–14

Read the text below and answer Questions 1–7.

Local campsites

A Prettycoat Farm

This well-known campsite in the wild near Browbourne is a winner with campers who are looking for time out from their fast-paced jobs in the capital. Despite its limited facilities, the site, with its large tent pitches, is an ideal base for exploring the area and driving to the rock museum, the craft workshops or Gaydon Castle. Just follow the signs.

B Newgammon Wild

This campsite looks like it's going to be a winner. It only opened last year, but already the website has some very positive reviews from the handful of campers who know about it so far. It offers splendid views over some of the country's most attractive beaches, which can be accessed by steep, narrow cliff steps. You need a good level of fitness for these, and don't forget to leave some energy for the return trip at the end of the day.

C Oakerly Estate

You won't be disappointed when you reach Oakerly, despite the problems of getting there by car on such narrow roads. You'll see quite a lot of motorhomes when you hit the clifftop, but there's still plenty of room for tents on the spacious lawn that also offers a camp kitchen, restaurant and bar. Make sure you stay safe and pitch your tent within the white line around the cliff edge, though.

D South Turnbull

The emphasis at this site is on back-to-basics camping. It's advisable to come in a group as there are few facilities and you need to do all your own cooking. The area is rather exposed, and in periods of bad weather it can't be reached at all so check on the website before you go.

E Boxer Trepis

The 20-metre high rockfaces that surround this site are especially attractive to rock climbers, who come here to camp from hundreds of miles away so that they can attempt the climb – and not always with success, according to the website! It's not compulsory, of course, and there are plenty of other activities for campers to get involved in, such as birdwatching and bathing in the sea.

Test 2

Questions 1–7

Look at the five descriptions of campsites, **A–E**, on page 39.

For which campsite are the following statements true?

Write the correct letter, **A–E**, in boxes 1–7 on your answer sheet.

NB You may use any letter more than once.

1   The site is impossible to get to at certain times.

2   It is in a convenient place for going by car to various tourist spots.

3   You should camp somewhere inside the marked zone.

4   Campers who enjoy a particular physical challenge come here.

5   The difficult journey to the site is worth the effort.

6   Few people have heard of this site.

7   Some physical effort is needed to enjoy nearby coastal areas.

Read the text below and answer Questions 8–14.

Durridge Heights (DH) Newsletter

Newsletter for people living in the seven-storey block of flats at Durridge Heights

Dear Residents

Water penetration

As a result of the recent heavy rains, water has seeped through the walls of some flats and reached a critical level. A decision has been taken to deal with this immediately. Scaffolding will be put up on the middle section of the southern wall, and the brickwork there will be sealed temporarily with a waterproof covering to prevent any further water getting in until the major building works take place next year.

Fire safety

Following our fire safety inspection, the front doors of individual flats were upgraded or replaced in order to satisfy fire safety regulations. As advised in the previous Newsletter, the decoration of the hall side of the front doors will be incorporated into the Fire Safety Project and will be carried out in due course by the company PRQ Builders.

Internal redecorations

The corridor walls on the inside of the building are redecorated every three years on a rolling basis and are being done this year. Please look out for signs indicating where the paint is wet. If you have children, make sure they keep away from the walls. DH cannot be held responsible for any spoilt clothing.

Air fresheners

We have received a small number of complaints about smells in the corridors. DH installed air fresheners some years ago. However, they were costly and the liquid in their spray stained the carpets. At present, we would prefer to ask residents to make sure smells cannot escape their front door and to seal rubbish bags when they put them in the corridor for collection and disposal by the caretaker.

Noise and DIY

While most leaseholders observe the regulations on noise, we have received complaints from others about out-of-hours drilling. Please note that any work involving hammers or electrical tools can only take place between 9.00 am and 5.30 pm on weekdays and between 9.00 am and 12.30 pm on a Saturday. There can be no exceptions to this rule. If you are planning to undertake such work during these hours, it is still polite to inform your neighbours of this so that they can make any necessary arrangements.

Test 2

Questions 8–14

Do the following statements agree with the information given in the text on page 41?

In boxes 8–14 on your answer sheet, write

> **TRUE** if the statement agrees with the information
> **FALSE** if the statement contradicts the information
> **NOT GIVEN** if there is no information on this

8   The water penetration in some flats is being treated as an emergency.

9   The southern wall will undergo a permanent repair this year.

10 Some people have failed to pay attention to 'wet paint' signs.

11 Air fresheners have caused some damage in the past.

12 Residents are responsible for removing their own rubbish from the building.

13 Some residents have reported problems with noisy neighbours.

14 DIY can take place outside the stated hours if your neighbour agrees.

SECTION 2   Questions 15–27

Read the text below and answer Questions 15–20.

A day in the life of a care worker

Care workers in Britain provide elderly and disabled people with the opportunity to remain independent at home, rather than moving into a care home. For those interested in the work, here is what a typical day could be like for a trained care worker.

Care workers often start early, as the first client of the day may need help getting out of bed and putting on their clothes; they may suffer from a condition that prevents them from doing this easily. Providing these services helps clients to look and feel as good as possible when beginning their day. The care worker may then help to cook breakfast for the client, and this is often a good time to enjoy a conversation and catch up on how they are feeling. Many clients appreciate being able to chat to someone regularly, as some may have no family members or friends living nearby. Next, the care worker may take the opportunity to do some basic housework for the client. Housework is often something that elderly people or people with disabilities may not be able to do themselves. Even something as simple as hoovering the living room can make a huge difference to a client's day. Of course, there may be the breakfast dishes to do as well.

Later in the morning, the care worker may move on to another client in order to help them prepare their midday meal. Care workers try to ensure this is healthy because it is so important to keep clients fit and well. When that's finished, the care worker may help the client to carry out their shopping by going with them to the local supermarket.

During the afternoon, a care worker may help a third client with an outdoor activity, which could involve going for a short walk in the local area or taking the laundry to the launderette. Elderly people may not feel confident going far on their own, so having company can be a great help.

The care worker may participate in cooking dinner with their last client and, before going home, they may also get out their client's medication. This ensures the client remembers to take it before going to bed.

Test 2

Questions 15–20

Complete the flowchart below.

Choose **ONE WORD ONLY** from the text for each answer.

Write your answers in boxes 15–20 on your answer sheet.

A day in the life of a care worker

It's an early start for the first client. You may have to help the client get up and dressed if they have a **15** .... that makes this challenging.

↓

The next task may be cooking breakfast and it's nice to have some **16** .... at this time.

↓

It may be a good idea to do some housework after this, such as **17** .... and washing up.

↓

You may then visit a second client and help them get a **18** .... lunch ready.

↓

Lunch may be followed by some **19** ....

↓

Afterwards, a third client may need help with an activity that involves going out of their home, such as doing their **20** ....

↓

You may cook dinner with the final client of the day and also remind them about their medication.

44

Read the text below and answer Questions 21–27.

How to find a good balance between your work and your personal life

A good work–life balance is beneficial to everyone. But how can it be achieved?

The first step is to take a serious look at the amount of time you are devoting to work and set about reducing it. The main benefit most people notice once they stop working too much is an improvement in their general health and wellbeing.

Tips for a healthy work–life balance

A recent study showed office workers spend approximately 1,700 hours a year in front of a computer. Ensure that your workstation is set up so you're as comfortable as possible and this will help to minimise the chance of any injuries.

Whether it's making a hot drink, going for a walk or simply chatting with a colleague, regular breaks are vital. Your brain needs a break roughly every 90 minutes or concentration declines, leaving you with difficulty focusing and feeling sleepy.

Setting goals for both your professional and personal life is great. Remember though, to make these realistic, because setting an unattainable goal is the quickest way to damage your confidence.

Activities such as sports and gymnastics are known to decrease tension and increase endurance, two important factors towards achieving a healthy work–life balance. They also boost your belief that you can do whatever you are faced with.

Sometimes it's easier said than done, but if you're juggling numerous pieces of work on a daily basis, learning to prioritise is key. Try to break down your work into various categories, depending on how urgent and important each piece of work is. This will help you to plan your day and achieve more.

Ensure you have time to do the things that make you happy. If you've got nothing nice to look forward to and can only see a long line of work days ahead of you, this can easily become overwhelming and ultimately hinder your productivity.

It's there for a reason and there are no prizes for giving it up, so make sure you take your annual holiday entitlement. You don't have to be going on an exotic foreign trip – maybe you just fancy a rest day watching films or you want to take some time off to spend with a friend you don't see enough.

Family, friends and favourite pets are the ultimate life enhancers. From evenings out to simply taking a walk in the sunshine, spending time with the ones you love is the best way to unwind fully and feel the effects of a good work–life balance.

Test 2

Questions 21–27

Complete the sentences below.

Choose **ONE WORD ONLY** from the text for each answer.

Write your answers in boxes 21–27 on your answer sheet.

21 People who cut down the hours they work gain most from feeling better physically and experiencing an increased sense of ....

22 It is important that those who work at desks avoid .... by checking their chair, work surface and screen are in the best position.

23 Having targets to work towards is useful but they should be ....

24 When there are many different tasks to do, the ability to .... them is vital.

25 People who give up all treats in their personal time may find their .... decreases.

26 It is wise to use the full amount of .... allowance every year.

27 Making time to do things with close companions, relatives or .... is a great way to relax.

SECTION 3   Questions 28–40

Read the text below and answer Questions 28–40.

City's 'Henry' programme gives children choices while helping parents stay in the driving seat

Leeds has become the first city in the UK to report a drop in childhood obesity after introducing a programme called 'Henry' to help parents set boundaries for their children and put them off sweets and junk food. Only a few cities in the world, notably Amsterdam, have managed to cut child obesity. As in Amsterdam, the decline in Leeds is most marked among families living in the most deprived areas, where the problem is worst and hardest to tackle.

'The improvement in the most deprived children in Leeds is startling,' said Susan Jebb, a professor of diet and population health at Oxford University, whose team has analysed the city's data. Over four years, obesity has dropped from 11.5% to 10.5% and the trajectory is steadily downwards. Among the more affluent families, there was also a decline from 6.8% to 6%. Overall the drop was from 9.4% to 8.8%. The data comes from the national child measurement programme (NCMP), which requires all children to be weighed at the start and end of primary school. The biggest decline in obesity in Leeds is 6.4% in the reception class, at about the age of four.

No such data has been reported elsewhere in the UK, where childhood obesity is a major concern. The measurement programme shares the progress made in each city with those considered comparable. For Leeds, the 15 closest 'neighbours' at the start of its study period in 2009 were Sheffield, Kirklees, Bristol, Newcastle upon Tyne, Coventry, Bolton, Wakefield, Derby, Bradford, Dudley, Medway, Liverpool, Swindon, County Durham and Warrington. The obesity rates there and across the country have not shifted. Susan Jebb added that the dropping rate in Leeds appeared to be a trend. 'This is four years, not one rogue data point,' she said at the European Congress on Obesity in Glasgow where she presented the research.

Jebb, a former government adviser, says they cannot be sure what has turned the tide in Leeds – but it could involve a programme called 'Henry' that the city introduced as the core of its obesity strategy in 2009, focusing particularly on the youngest children and poorest families. 'Henry' (Health, Exercise, Nutrition for the Really Young) supports parents in setting boundaries for their children and taking a positive stance on issues from healthy eating to bedtimes.

'Henry's' chief executive, Kim Roberts, said the drop in obesity in Leeds was 'unprecedented … The indicators are that this isn't happening in other cities'. The programme encourages authoritative rather than authoritarian parenting, she said. 'Authoritarian parenting is when children are told what to eat and what to do, such as being banned from leaving the table until they have eaten their sprouts,' said Roberts. 'Permissive parenting is asking children what they want to do. But 'Henry' encourages a third approach known as authoritative parenting, where parents make it clear they are in charge, but also respond to their children.' Instead of being asked what vegetable they want with dinner, children might be asked whether they would like carrots or broccoli. Instead of being told to go to bed, they are asked where they want to read their story beforehand.

Lisa, who joined a 'Henry' parenting course when her oldest daughter was two, is enthusiastic about her family's experience of the programme. She learned a lot about healthy eating, saved money by planning meals and lost two stone herself. 'I think it made me a better parent because of all the parenting skills stuff. I was able to share some of the ideas with my partner and as a result the kids became calmer and happier, which helped us feel less stressed too,' she said.

Janice Burberry, the head of public health at Leeds city council, said the early years were a good time to intervene to support families. 'Parents want to do the best for their children,' she said. 'We wanted to focus on prevention because it's very, very difficult when obesity has taken hold to tackle it. We understand that there is no magic bullet here. Parents are experts in their own lives, and they know what they can and can't achieve. The strategy of 'Henry' is about sitting alongside parents and thinking through what's right for them.'

The public health minister, Seema Kennedy, was enthusiastic. 'There are some fantastic pockets of work happening in early years already, and while still in the early phases, it is encouraging to see what can be achieved locally through interventions like this,' she said. 'I know how hard it can be for busy parents to make healthy choices for their families, so anything that can make it easier is a real lifeline.'

Questions 28–31

*Choose the correct letter, **A**, **B**, **C** or **D**.*

Write the correct letter in boxes 28–31 on your answer sheet.

28 In the first paragraph, what does the writer say about Amsterdam?

    A   Its 'Henry' programme was recommended to Leeds experts.
    B   It was the first world city to reduce obesity levels in children.
    C   It has experienced more severe childhood obesity levels than Leeds.
    D   Its pattern of success in cutting childhood obesity is like that of Leeds.

29 How did Susan Jebb respond to the fall in childhood obesity among poorer children in Leeds?

    A   She said she had expected it.
    B   She said she was amazed by the figures.
    C   She wanted to review some of her team's data.
    D   She felt some results were more interesting than others.

30 According to the writer, the NCMP data indicate that

    A   children should be weighed more frequently.
    B   most primary school children need to lose weight.
    C   children from wealthy families have less weight to lose than others.
    D   the youngest children show the highest levels of weight loss.

31 What links the 15 places listed in the third paragraph?

    A   They are not representative of the country overall.
    B   They all joined the 'Henry' programme at the same time.
    C   Their childhood obesity levels have remained the same since 2009.
    D   They are battling childhood obesity in a different way from Leeds.

Test 2

Questions 32–35

Look at the following statements (Questions 32–35) and the list of people below.

Match each statement with the correct person, **A**, **B**, **C** or **D**.

Write the correct letter, **A**, **B**, **C** or **D**, in boxes 32–35 on your answer sheet.

NB You may use any letter more than once.

32 The aim in Leeds was to take steps to stop weight gain among children before it became a real problem.

33 Childhood obesity levels in Leeds have fallen consistently over a period of time.

34 Something that simplifies the struggle to get children to eat well is very helpful to parents.

35 Parents in general are realistic about their potential to make changes to their children's lifestyle.

List of People
A Susan Jebb
B Kim Roberts
C Janice Burberry
D Seema Kennedy

Questions 36–39

Complete the summary below.

Choose **ONE WORD ONLY** from the text for each answer.

Write your answers in boxes 36–39 on your answer sheet.

The 'Henry' programme

'Henry' was used in Leeds from 2009 in the fight against childhood obesity. The programme focuses on situations such as mealtimes and bedtimes, and it encourages parents to set firm **36** .... during these periods.

According to Kim Roberts, 'Henry' aims to help people become more **37** .... as parents. In this way, they do not instruct children to do things, nor give them total freedom of choice as in a **38** .... parenting style. Instead, they allow children to make some decisions for themselves. This might be a choice of vegetable at the dinner table or a decision about where a **39** .... should be enjoyed in the evening.

Lisa, a parent who joined the programme, felt enthusiastic about her children's responses to it and the effect it had overall on her family.

Question 40

Choose the correct letter, **A**, **B**, **C** or **D**.

Write the correct letter in box 40 on your answer sheet.

Which title is the most suitable for the text?

- **A** A look at what 'Henry' has achieved in Leeds
- **B** 'Henry's the best,' according to Leeds children
- **C** Leeds parents discuss how 'Henry' has helped them
- **D** It's all about saying 'no', according to 'Henry'

Test 2

WRITING

WRITING TASK 1

You should spend about 20 minutes on this task.

> *You are a member of an International Students' club. The club is organising an event to celebrate popular food from around the world.*
>
> *Write a letter to the event organiser, Luis. In your letter*
> - *offer to make a popular dish from your country*
> - *describe what this dish is*
> - *explain why it should be included in the event*

Write at least 150 words.

You do **NOT** need to write any addresses.

Begin your letter as follows:

Dear Luis,

WRITING TASK 2

You should spend about 40 minutes on this task.

Write about the following topic:

> *It is sometimes possible to pay somebody to do things you don't want to do, or don't have time to do, for example, household chores or looking after children.*
>
> *Is this a good way of providing work for others?*
>
> *Should people do these things themselves?*

Give reasons for your answer and include any relevant examples from your own knowledge or experience.

Write at least 250 words.

Test 2

SPEAKING

PART 1

The examiner asks you about yourself, your home, work or studies and other familiar topics.

EXAMPLE

Travelling by plane

- Have you travelled a lot by plane? [To where?/Why not?]
- Why do you think some people enjoy travelling by plane?
- Would you like to live near an airport? [Why/Why not?]
- In the future, do you think that you will travel by plane more often? [Why/Why not?]

PART 2

Describe a person from your country who has won a prize, award or medal.

You should say:
   who this person is
   which prize, award or medal they received
   what they did to win this

and explain whether you think it was right that this person received this prize, award or medal.

You will have to talk about the topic for one to two minutes. You have one minute to think about what you are going to say. You can make some notes to help you if you wish.

PART 3

Discussion topics:

Rewards for children at school

Example questions:
What types of school prizes do children in your country receive?
What do you think are the advantages of rewarding schoolchildren for good work?
Do you agree that it's more important for children to receive rewards from their parents than from teachers?

Rewards for sportspeople

Example questions:
Do you think that some sportspeople (e.g. top footballers) are paid too much money?
Should everyone on a team get the same prize money when they win?
Do you agree with the view that, in sport, taking part is more important than winning?

Test 3

LISTENING

PART 1   *Questions 1–10*

Questions 1–6

Complete the notes below.

Write **ONE WORD AND/OR A NUMBER** for each answer.

Local food shops

Where to go

- Kite Place – near the **1** ....

Fish market

- cross the **2** .... and turn right

- best to go before **3** .... pm, earlier than closing time

Organic shop

- called **4** '...'

- below a restaurant in the large, grey building

- look for the large **5** .... outside

Supermarket

- take a **6** .... minibus, number 289

Test 3

Questions 7–10

Complete the table below.

Write **ONE WORD ONLY** for each answer.

	Shopping	
	To buy	**Other ideas**
Fish market	a dozen prawns	a handful of **7** .... (type of seaweed)
Organic shop	beans and a **8** .... for dessert	spices and **9** ....
Bakery	a brown loaf	a **10** .... tart

PART 2   Questions 11–20

Questions 11–16

What information is given about each of the following festival workshops?

Choose **SIX** answers from the box and write the correct letter, **A–H**, next to Questions 11–16.

	Information
A	involves painting and drawing
B	will be led by a prize-winning author
C	is aimed at children with a disability
D	involves a drama activity
E	focuses on new relationships
F	is aimed at a specific age group
G	explores an unhappy feeling
H	raises awareness of a particular culture

Festival workshops

11 Superheroes   ....
12 Just do it   ....
13 Count on me   ....
14 Speak up   ....
15 Jump for joy   ....
16 Sticks and stones ....

Test 3

Questions 17 and 18

Choose **TWO** letters, **A–E**.

Which **TWO** reasons does the speaker give for recommending *Alive and Kicking*?

- **A** It will appeal to both boys and girls.
- **B** The author is well known.
- **C** It has colourful illustrations.
- **D** It is funny.
- **E** It deals with an important topic.

Questions 19 and 20

Choose **TWO** letters, **A–E**.

Which **TWO** pieces of advice does the speaker give to parents about reading?

- **A** Encourage children to write down new vocabulary.
- **B** Allow children to listen to audio books.
- **C** Get recommendations from librarians.
- **D** Give children a choice about what they read.
- **E** Only read aloud to children until they can read independently.

Listening

PART 3   Questions 21–30

Questions 21–25

Choose the correct letter, A, B or C.

Science experiment for Year 12 students

21   How does Clare feel about the students in her Year 12 science class?

   A   worried that they are not making progress
   B   challenged by their poor behaviour in class
   C   frustrated at their lack of interest in the subject

22   How does Jake react to Clare's suggestion about an experiment based on children's diet?

   A   He is concerned that the results might not be meaningful.
   B   He feels some of the data might be difficult to obtain.
   C   He suspects that the conclusions might be upsetting.

23   What problem do they agree may be involved in an experiment involving animals?

   A   Any results may not apply to humans.
   B   It may be complicated to get permission.
   C   Students may not be happy about animal experiments.

24   What question do they decide the experiment should address?

   A   Are mice capable of controlling their food intake?
   B   Does an increase in sugar lead to health problems?
   C   How much do supplements of different kinds affect health?

25   Clare might also consider doing another experiment involving

   A   other types of food supplement.
   B   different genetic strains of mice.
   C   varying amounts of exercise.

Questions 26–30

Complete the flowchart below.

Choose **FIVE** answers from the box and write the correct letter, **A–H**, next to Questions 26–30.

A	size
B	escape
C	age
D	water
E	cereal
F	calculations
G	changes
H	colour

Choose mice which are all the same **26** ....

↓

Divide the mice into two groups, each with a different **27** ....

↓

Put each group in a separate cage.
Feed group A commercial mouse food.
Feed group B the same, but also sugar contained in **28** ....

↓

Take measurements using an electronic scale.
Place them in a weighing chamber to prevent **29** ....

↓

Do all necessary **30** ....

PART 4   Questions 31–40

Complete the notes below.

Write **ONE WORD ONLY** for each answer.

Microplastics

Where microplastics come from

- fibres from some **31** .... during washing
- the breakdown of large pieces of plastic
- waste from industry
- the action of vehicle tyres on roads

Effects of microplastics

- They cause injuries to the **32** .... of wildlife and affect their digestive systems.
- They enter the food chain, e.g., in bottled and tap water, **33** .... and seafood.
- They may not affect human health, but they are already banned in skin cleaning products and **34** .... in some countries.
- Microplastics enter the soil through the air, rain and **35** ....

Microplastics in the soil – a study by Anglia Ruskin University

- Earthworms are important because they add **36** .... to the soil.
- The study aimed to find whether microplastics in earthworms affect the **37** .... of plants.
- The study found that microplastics caused:
  - **38** .... loss in earthworms
  - fewer seeds to germinate
  - a rise in the level of **39** .... in the soil.

The study concluded:
  - soil should be seen as an important natural process.
  - changes to soil damage both ecosystems and **40** ....

READING

SECTION 1 Questions 1–14

Read the text below and answer Questions 1–8.

A Purple Rainbow: The Truth

Having actors playing popular rock band *Purple Rainbow* seemed like a bad idea, but in fact they're impressive musicians themselves. Their fans in the film were actual fans of the group and transferred their enthusiasm to the actors very convincingly. I assumed there would be plenty of music, linked by weak dialogue, but I was wrong. And the support that band members gave to lead singer Jerry Cosgrove when tragedy entered his life had me close to tears, giving me a new appreciation of the band.

B Home Fires

I expected a standard, rather dull, story about domestic life, like the director's last two films. Instead, *Home Fires* had me on the edge of my seat with excitement. It's certainly worth a second viewing. Having said that, although it is apparently a film intended for all ages, many children would find the long discussions of relationship issues boring, and they contributed little or nothing to the film.

C The Jeffersons

One of the most popular films of the past half century is *Mary and Tom*, and a remake of it seems unnecessary. Nevertheless, *The Jeffersons* has some delightful elements, particularly the acting of Yvonne Richards. She really brought the character she played to life, but sadly, neither she nor the other actors could make the script sound natural.

D Space Challenge 5

This film makes an important ethical point about treating other people with respect, but that is likely to be missed by many teenagers, the target audience, as it assumes familiarity with the world as it was 20 years ago. With change happening so fast these days, many of the references will leave them confused.

E Uplands

Uplands could have been a delightful film: it has a charming story, witty dialogue, and is visually breathtaking. But the two lead actors are at their best in thrillers, not films like this one. James Petherick, who plays the hero, fails to gain the sympathy of the audience, who should be moved by the ups and downs in his life.

Reading

Questions 1–8

Look at the five film reviews, **A–E**, on page 62.

For which film review are the following statements true?

*Write the correct letter, **A–E**, in boxes 1–8 on your answer sheet.*

NB *You may use any letter more than once.*

1   The reviewer thinks some of the cast are unsuitable for their roles.
2   The dialogue in this film seems unrealistic.
3   The reviewer found this film unexpectedly emotional.
4   This film contains dialogue that is uninteresting for some viewers.
5   This film carries a moral message.
6   Non-actors take part in this film.
7   The reviewer thinks this film should be seen again.
8   This film mentions things that audience members won't know about.

Test 3

Read the text below and answer Questions 9–14.

Sports events in New Zealand

A   McLeans Island Run

This unique running and cycling event winds its way through the Canterbury countryside and finishes in Orana Park, where your spectators will include lions, tigers, gorillas and giraffes. Whether you're a first-timer or a seasoned professional, there's a distance to suit you. Choose from the short, the sprint or the standard distance. You can race to help other people too – if you get some friends or workmates to take part, you'll be in with a chance to win $25,000 to put towards a good cause of your choice.

B   The Pioneer

The Pioneer is an awe-inspiring seven-day mountain bike race through New Zealand's pristine Southern Alps. It is the first race of its kind to link together over 500 km of farm tracks, cycle trails, double track and single track riding in a very special part of the world where soaring mountain peaks, crystal-clear lakes, and high country await. If you're looking for a mountain bike race to get you inspired, this is it!

C   Race Drive Experience

If you have ever wanted to experience the extreme thrill of driving a 6000cc race car, then this is definitely for you! You start off your Race Drive Experience by meeting the skilled team of racing drivers at the Motorsport Park Raceway, before being fully kitted out with one of our race suits and safety helmet. Then you are strapped into the passenger seat of one of our racing cars and taken on a demo drive, covering racing lines, braking points and race driving tricks. Finally you take the driver's seat and can undertake your own high-speed laps of the circuit.

D   Banks Peninsular Walking Festival

The Banks Peninsula Walking Festival offers guided walks all over the Banks Peninsula. The guides, all volunteers, are local people who love to share their passion for this special place with those from the wider community. Participants are guaranteed an enjoyable experience as they relax, get to know new people and absorb the stories and atmosphere of this fantastic land.

Questions 9–14

Look at the four advertisements for sports events, **A–D**, on page 64.

For which event are the following statements true?

Write the correct letter, **A–D**, in boxes 9–14 on your answer sheet.

NB You may use any letter more than once.

9   You see spectacular scenery.
10 You are provided with special clothing.
11 You may be watched while you are doing the activity.
12 You watch someone else before doing the activity yourself.
13 You meet people who are expert at the activity.
14 You can raise money for a charity.

SECTION 2   Questions 15–27

Read the text below and answer Questions 15–21.

What to do if you are made redundant

Employees are made redundant when a company has to reduce the workforce because a job or jobs are no longer needed. It has nothing to do with the employees' ability to do their jobs. However, dealing with redundancy can be difficult. Here are some tips on how to cope.

First of all, don't panic. It's common for people to either rush into a flurry of activity or be frozen by the shock of being suddenly made redundant. The best course of action is to keep calm and draw up a list of all of the things you need to arrange in the months ahead. It's important to find out what your rights are. Obtain a copy of the in-house redundancy policy if there is one and check out your contract for exit terms.

Try to maintain good relations wherever possible with your employer, even if you are angry about the manner of your exit. You will still need a reasonable reference when the time comes to move on, and it may be that your boss can make useful introductions or offer you consultancy work.

Help from a professional outplacement company can make a huge difference to your job search success and reduce the amount of time taken to find your next role. You can purchase this yourself, but there are advantages to having it arranged via your company.

Don't rush into applying for any or every job that comes up. Take stock of what you have to offer, what you want to do, and carry out in-depth research to find out what employers are actually looking for. Talk to people in your target industry for career advice and information. This information will be invaluable in helping you identify potential employers.

Assess whether there are any gaps in experience or qualifications that could be a barrier to getting another job and address them. Enrol on some of those courses you have always been too busy to go on: not only will this enhance your skills, it also shows your commitment to continuous professional development.

Redundancy enables you to move your career forward in line with your own personal agenda. Although it can be traumatic, many people find that redundancy is actually the incentive they need to take their career in the direction they actually want to go. So think about what you really want, and go for it.

Questions 15–21

Complete the notes below.

Choose **ONE WORD ONLY** from the text for each answer.

Write your answers in boxes 15–21 on your answer sheet.

Dealing with redundancy

Initial steps

Start by considering what needs to be done and make a **15** .... to work through.

Get the company's policy concerning laying off staff and check personal work-related documents.

Dealing with the company

Avoid letting the management see you are annoyed because:

- you want to receive a positive **16** .... from them for a future post.
- you might get some **17** .... projects from them in the future.

Moving on

Find an organisation that specialises in **18** .... to help you look for another job.

Invest time in doing serious **19** .... concerning the current requirements in your sector.

Consider if your work and training records contain **20** .... that might prevent you finding work.

Sign up for any relevant courses to improve your chances of being selected for a new post.

Conclusion

Look on redundancy as a useful **21** .... to advance, rather than the end of your career.

Read the text below and answer Questions 22–27.

Palvin's Restaurant

Instructions to new kitchen staff

Dress standards at our restaurants are extremely important whichever area you work in. The following information will help ensure that you have a professional appearance every day as you carry out your foodservice duties.

Palvin's Restaurant chain provides new kitchen staff with their uniforms and you are advised to come to work with a note of your chest, waist and hip measurements to assist in this process. On your first day, you'll be issued with two pairs of trousers, two aprons, two jackets and two hats. Once you're happy that you have the correct size, please take the garments home and add a name tag to each one. Put these inside the garments so that they cannot be seen.

Kitchen work can be messy, and it is up to you to make sure that your uniform is kept clean, but you will receive a laundry allowance to help you do this. Towels are available at work, but it's a good idea to bring your own too in case you need it. You can keep this and any other personal items safe in the lockers that are available for use while you're on duty. It's advisable to bring your own small padlock for these.

Uniforms should not be worn outside work. You should wear your normal clothes to and from work but make sure they're respectable. For example, hoodies and other similar tops are not acceptable in the kitchens; if it's cold, wear a jacket. When you arrive at work, you can use the changing facilities located next to the lockers to put on your uniform. You can wear your own shoes in the kitchens as long as they're sturdy and enclosed. We strongly recommend rubber soles so that they do not slip on the floor.

If you incur any injuries that require crutches while you're working for the company, you cannot then take on any tasks that involve standing up. However, if such a situation should occur, we will make every effort to place you in an appropriate area where you can sit down to work so you will not need to take time off. Employees who have smaller injuries, such as hand cuts, need to check with their manager whether they can come to work: you may have to take time off to avoid infection.

Reading

Questions 22–27

Complete the sentences below.

Choose **NO MORE THAN TWO WORDS** from the text for each answer.

Write your answers in boxes 22–27 on your answer sheet.

22 New staff must record their own body …………………………………… before arriving at work.

23 You should use your …………………………………… to ensure that your uniform is never dirty.

24 Clothes worn to travel to work must be …………………………………… .

25 Casual wear, such as …………………………………… , should not be worn in the kitchen area.

26 Staff using …………………………………… may still come to work.

27 Please contact the manager before arriving at the kitchens if you have any …………………………………… or other similar injuries.

Test 3

SECTION 3   Questions 28–40

Read the text below and answer Questions 28–40.

The forgotten role of women in medieval arts

A   A team of archaeologists recently and unexpectedly revealed direct archaeological evidence of the involvement of medieval women in the production of manuscripts. This challenges the widespread assumptions that men were the sole producers of books throughout the period in European history known as the Middle Ages (600–1500 AD). They did so by identifying particles of blue pigment in the fossilised dental plaque of a medieval woman as lapis lazuli, an extremely valuable stone at the time. The findings are the first of their kind and strongly suggest it will be possible to increase the profile of ancient female artists in the historical and archaeological record by analysing their dirty teeth.

B   This discovery was made possible by applying technological advances in the field of archaeological science to a little-studied deposit on teeth known as tartar, which is mineralised dental plaque. In most societies today, oral hygiene practices are part of our daily routine, meaning that dental plaque is regularly removed and doesn't have a chance to build up on our teeth. This was not the case in the past. Plaque built up and mineralised over the course of people's lives. This solid deposit has unique archaeological potential. A key characteristic of dental plaque is that while it forms it has the ability to entrap a wide range of microscopic and molecular debris that enters a person's mouth. When dental plaque hardens and becomes tartar, it can entomb these particles and molecules for hundreds or thousands of years – potentially even millions.

C   The majority of scholarly work conducted on ancient tartar has been centred on what people ate but, besides taking in food, the human mouth is subject to a constant influx of particles of different types directly from the environment. Tree and grass pollen, spores, cotton fibres, medicinal plants and micro-charcoal have all been reported among the finds from this type of dental analysis. Despite such promising evidence, the value of tartar as environmental evidence has not, so far, been much exploited.

D The team analysed the skeletal remains of a female individual, known as B78, who lived in the 11th–12th century. She was buried in the grounds of a former women's monastery in Dalheim, Germany, that is in ruins today but was occupied by various religious groups for around a thousand years. They found well over 100 bright blue particles, in the form of small crystals and individual flecks, scattered throughout the tartar which was still preserved on her teeth. Her skeletal remains had not indicated anything particular about her life, besides a general indication that she probably did not do any hard labour. The blue particles were unlike any other discovery – firstly because of their colour, and secondly because of their sheer number.

E To be sure about the nature of the particles of bright blue powder trapped in the woman's tartar, a range of microscopy techniques were used. All techniques provided the same results: the blue specks were lazurite, the blue portion of the lapis lazuli stone, a substance more precious than gold in Medieval Europe. Afghanistan was the only source of the stone at the time, and the preparation of the pigment took great skill.

F So how did particles of this precious material end up deposited on this woman's teeth? A variety of reasons were possible, from painting to accidental ingestion during pigment preparation, or even the consumption of the powder as a medicine. But the way in which the blue particles were found in her tartar – single flecks in different areas – pointed to repeated exposure, not a single intake. And creating a vivid blue pigment from lapis lazuli required an Arabic method of oil flotation that did not appear in European artists' manuals until after the 15th century. This all suggests that it's more likely that this ultramarine pigment was brought into the region as a finished product for use by artists.

G The most likely explanation, then, is that this was an artist who repeatedly used her lips to make a fine point on the end of her brush in order to paint intricate detail on manuscripts. This finding suggests that women were more involved in the production of books throughout the Middle Ages than tends to be thought. Before the 12th century fewer than one per cent of the books that still remain can be traced to the work of women. Additionally, artists are largely invisible in both the historic and archaeological records as they rarely signed their work before the 15th century and, until now, there have been no known skeletal markers directly associated with producing art. The work strongly points to the possibility of using microscopic particles entombed in ancient tartar to track the artists of ancient times. It also suggests that it may be possible to track other 'dusty' crafts using this method and thereby reveal the invisible workforce behind many forms of art.

Test 3

Questions 28–32

Choose the correct letter, **A**, **B**, **C** or **D**.

Write the correct letter in boxes 28–32 on your answer sheet.

28   In Paragraph A, what does the writer say about the archaeology team's work?

   A   It confirmed what they had assumed when they started it.
   B   It was hard to persuade other historians about their findings.
   C   It could reveal the importance of various women in history.
   D   It could help identify the number of books written in the Middle Ages.

29   What point does the writer make about dental tartar in Paragraph C?

   A   Archaeologists could make more use of it than they do at present.
   B   Some particles are more easily trapped in it than others.
   C   The environment can cause it to break down.
   D   Changes in people's diet have influenced its composition.

30   What did the skeleton of B78 suggest about her?

   A   She had not been very old when she died.
   B   Her life had not been very physically demanding.
   C   Her teeth had more tartar than most skeletons of that age.
   D   She had been given a grander burial than other women of her time.

31   What is the writer doing in Paragraph F?

   A   supporting the team's view that the blue pigment was imported
   B   explaining why artists in Europe liked to use the blue pigment
   C   comparing artistic designs using the blue pigment in different parts of the world
   D   criticising arguments put forward by other scientists about the blue pigment

32   What problem does the writer highlight about medieval artists in Paragraph G?

   A   the poor facilities available to females in the profession
   B   the small number of projects available to them
   C   the difficulties locating their skeletal remains for study
   D   the lack of evidence for their contribution to books

Questions 33–36

The text on pages 70 and 71 has seven paragraphs, **A–G**.

Which paragraph mentions the following?

*Write the correct letter, **A–G**, in boxes 33–36 on your answer sheet.*

33 reference to the possible length of time that tartar can preserve particles from the air

34 two reasons why the particles that the team found in teeth were unique

35 various examples of the types of particle that can be discovered in old teeth

36 a suggestion that the blue pigment might have been used in medieval times to cure illness

Questions 37–40

Complete the summary below.

*Choose **ONE WORD ONLY** from the text for each answer.*

Write your answers in boxes 37–40 on your answer sheet.

Lapis lazuli

A blue pigment used to create artworks in Europe in the Middle Ages was derived from a stone called lapis lazuli. In medieval times, even **37** .... was not as valuable. Lapis lazuli could only be found in Afghanistan and a lot of **38** .... was needed to make the pigment from the stone.

The procedure used to do this appeared much later in the manuals used by European artists and this suggests that the product came to their countries as an imported powder. Artists often had to make a **39** .... on their brushes using their mouths, which then enabled them to produce the fine features needed for **40** .... and books.

Test 3

WRITING

WRITING TASK 1

You should spend about 20 minutes on this task.

> *Five months ago, you started renting an apartment on a six-month agreement. You now wish to stay in the apartment for longer than the six months you originally agreed with the owner.*
>
> *Write a letter to the owner of your apartment. In your letter*
> - *say how long you now want to rent the apartment for*
> - *explain why your plans have changed*
> - *tell the owner about a problem in the apartment*

Write at least 150 words.

You do **NOT** need to write any addresses.

Begin your letter as follows:

Dear .... ,

WRITING TASK 2

You should spend about 40 minutes on this task.

Write about the following topic:

> **Some consumers are increasingly choosing to buy goods that are produced in their local area, rather than imported goods.**
>
> **What are the reasons for this?**
>
> **Is this a positive or a negative trend?**

Give reasons for your answer and include any relevant examples from your own knowledge or experience.

Write at least 250 words.

Test 3

SPEAKING

PART 1

The examiner asks you about yourself, your home, work or studies and other familiar topics.

EXAMPLE

Holidays

- Do you prefer spending holidays with friends or with family? [Why?]
- What kind of holiday accommodation do you like to stay in? [Why?]
- What plans do you have for your next holiday?
- Is your city or region a good place for other people to visit on holiday? [Why/Why not?]

PART 2

> **Describe a car journey you made that took longer than expected.**
>
> You should say:
> where you were going
> who you were with
> how you felt during the journey
>
> and explain why this car journey took longer than expected.

You will have to talk about the topic for one to two minutes. You have one minute to think about what you are going to say. You can make some notes to help you if you wish.

PART 3

Discussion topics:

Driving a car

Example questions:
How interested are young people in your country in learning to drive?
What are the differences between driving in the countryside and driving in the city?
Do you consider most drivers where you live to be good drivers?

Electric cars

Example questions:
How popular are electric cars in your country?
In what ways could more people be persuaded to buy electric cars?
Do you think all cars will be electric one day?

Test 4

LISTENING

PART 1   Questions 1–10

Questions 1–6

Complete the notes below.

*Write **ONE WORD AND/OR A NUMBER** for each answer.*

First day at work

- Name of supervisor: **1** ....
- Where to leave coat and bag: use **2** .... in staffroom
- See Tiffany in HR: to give **3** .... number
- to collect **4** ....
- Location of HR office: on **5** .... floor
- Supervisor's mobile number: **6** ....

Questions 7–10

Complete the table below.

*Write **ONE WORD ONLY** for each answer.*

Responsibilities			
	Task 1	**Task 2**	**Notes**
Bakery section	Check sell-by dates	Change price labels	Use **7** .... labels
Sushi takeaway counter	Re-stock with **8** .... boxes if needed	Wipe preparation area and clean the sink	Do not clean any knives
Meat and fish counters	Clean the serving area, including the weighing scales	Collect **9** .... for the fish from the cold-room	Must wear special **10** ....

Test 4

PART 2   Questions 11–20

Questions 11 and 12

Choose **TWO** letters, **A–E**.

Which **TWO** problems with some training programmes for new runners does Liz mention?

- A   There is a risk of serious injury.
- B   They are unsuitable for certain age groups.
- C   They are unsuitable for people with health issues.
- D   It is difficult to stay motivated.
- E   There is a lack of individual support.

Questions 13 and 14

Choose **TWO** letters, **A–E**.

Which **TWO** tips does Liz recommend for new runners?

- A   doing two runs a week
- B   running in the evening
- C   going on runs with a friend
- D   listening to music during runs
- E   running very slowly

Questions 15–18

What reason prevented each of the following members of the Compton Park Runners Club from joining until recently?

*Write the correct letter, **A**, **B**, or **C** next to Questions 15–18.*

	Reasons
A	a lack of confidence
B	a dislike of running
C	a lack of time

Club members

15 Ceri   ....

16 James   ....

17 Leo   ....

18 Mark   ....

Questions 19 and 20

*Choose the correct letter, **A**, **B** or **C**.*

19 What does Liz say about running her first marathon?

    A   It had always been her ambition.
    B   Her husband persuaded her to do it.
    C   She nearly gave up before the end.

20 Liz says new runners should sign up for a race

    A   every six months.
    B   within a few weeks of taking up running.
    C   after completing several practice runs.

Test 4

PART 3   Questions 21–30

Questions 21–25

Choose the correct letter, **A**, **B** or **C**.

21   Kieran thinks the packing advice given by Jane's grandfather is

   A   common sense.
   B   hard to follow.
   C   over-protective.

22   How does Jane feel about the books her grandfather has given her?

   A   They are not worth keeping.
   B   They should go to a collector.
   C   They have sentimental value for her.

23   Jane and Kieran agree that hardback books should be

   A   put out on display.
   B   given as gifts to visitors.
   C   more attractively designed.

24   While talking about taking a book from a shelf, Jane

   A   describes the mistakes other people make doing it.
   B   reflects on a significant childhood experience.
   C   explains why some books are easier to remove than others.

25   What do Jane and Kieran suggest about new books?

   A   Their parents liked buying them as presents.
   B   They would like to buy more of them.
   C   Not everyone can afford them.

Questions 26–30

Where does Jane's grandfather keep each of the following types of books in his shop?

Choose **FIVE** *answers from the box and write the correct letter,* **A–G**, *next to Questions 26–30.*

Location of books	
A	near the entrance
B	in the attic
C	at the back of the shop
D	on a high shelf
E	near the stairs
F	in a specially designed space
G	within the café

Types of books

26 rare books   ....

27 children's books   ....

28 unwanted books   ....

29 requested books   ....

30 coursebooks   ....

PART 4   Questions 31–40

Complete the notes below.

Write **ONE WORD ONLY** for each answer.

Tree planting

Reforestation projects should:

- include a range of tree species
- not include invasive species because of possible **31** .... with native species
- aim to capture carbon, protect the environment and provide sustainable sources of **32** .... for local people
- use tree seeds with a high genetic diversity to increase resistance to **33** .... and climate change
- plant trees on previously forested land which is in a bad condition, not select land which is being used for **34** ....

Large-scale reforestation projects

- Base planning decisions on information from accurate **35** ....
- Drones are useful for identifying areas in Brazil which are endangered by keeping **36** .... and illegal logging.

Lampang Province, Northern Thailand

- A forest was restored in an area damaged by mining.
- A variety of native fig trees were planted, which are important for
  - supporting many wildlife species
  - increasing the **37** .... of recovery by attracting animals and birds, e.g., **38** .... were soon attracted to the area.

Involving local communities

- Destruction of mangrove forests in Madagascar made it difficult for people to make a living from **39** ....
- The mangrove reforestation project:
  - provided employment for local people
  - restored a healthy ecosystem
  - protects against the higher risk of **40** ....

READING

SECTION 1 Questions 1–14

Read the text below and answer Questions 1–5.

Customer reviews of cafés in the town of Artingly

A Coffee Dream

The décor of this café is great, but why don't the owners make it easier to queue up? There's so little space around the counter that everyone is squashed together when they order. I'd also recommend checking that there's somewhere to sit when you go in as it can get very crowded.

B Cafélingo

Local media are right in saying that this café makes the best cup of coffee in town, but remember to take the time to appreciate the local artwork displayed on the walls around you while you're sipping your cappuccino.

C Billy Ding's Café

As this café had been recommended by someone staying in our hotel, we decided to try it out. Despite being on the first floor, it was already crowded by ten in the morning, and it quickly became clear to us that this is a place that residents in the area use regularly. Fortunately, a family group left just as we arrived, and we were lucky enough to get a table overlooking the street. There we enjoyed some delicious pancakes, which we washed down with the biggest 'small' coffee we've ever had!

D Drink in the Park

No one can deny that this coffee house is located in a beautiful setting. If the outside tables are full, you can simply take your cup of coffee over to one of the many park benches and enjoy it there, which is what we often do.

E Chocolotta's

We've been here several times and always order the same drinks and food. The last few times, however, we've noticed that the rolls have less filling and the coffee tastes watery. Perhaps the company is trying to cut costs, but this will only lead to customers going elsewhere.

F   Café Soloist

After a considerable search, we eventually found Café Soloist tucked away behind an organic grocery store. There was nothing outside to indicate that it was there, which would have been helpful! Once inside, we were presented with a menu that had more coffee options than we had ever seen before. Twenty minutes and a lot of discussion later, we finally decided what we wanted. We could then sit back and enjoy the happy chatter and welcoming atmosphere around us.

Questions 1–5

Look at the six reviews of cafés in the town of Artlingly, **A–F**, on pages 83 and above.

For which café are the following statements true?

Write the correct letter, **A–F**, in boxes 1–5 on your answer sheet.

NB You may use any letter more than once.

1   Cup sizes are more generous than you might expect.
2   Recent changes are likely to have a negative impact.
3   It needs better signage for customers.
4   It has a strong local customer base.
5   It deserves the public praise it has received.

Read the text below and answer Questions 6–14.

Frog Valley development

Creating a better area to meet the needs of the local community

The proposal to develop the part of our city known as Frog Valley has now been passed to the local council for consideration and approval. In case you missed earlier newspaper reports, here briefly are some of the changes and improvements that are being planned for the site.

An area of land in the south-east corner of Frog Valley has been allocated to the construction of a new primary school which, if building does go ahead, will accommodate 300 children. The size and location of the school mean that admission will not be limited to families who live in the area.

Another feature that will bring people together will be the new shopping mall. Plans are to move all the existing local shops, which are currently located in small groups around the site, into one shopping zone, and this will see the addition of an organic farm shop and a vegan store.

A community centre will be central to the development of the site. It will provide a much needed meeting place for clubs and societies that, until now, have had to meet wherever they can find a venue. The pride of the centre will be a multi-gym with swimming pool – something younger residents have been requesting for some time but that has never been possible, due to cost.

For many years now, local businesspeople have been asking for better business premises, and this is now a priority for Frog Valley. Twenty thousand square metres of space will be used to house anything from small startups to large existing local businesses. It will be built to the south-east of the site, with dedicated car parking for office workers, either within each office area or in a single car park.

At our public consultation meeting, some residents asked if it would be possible to include services such as dentistry and various types of medical testing facilities within the health centre. This would mean adding to the existing building and there are no plans to do this at present. However, it will be possible to see a doctor at weekends and in the evenings, which is a welcome development.

Test 4

Questions 6–14

Do the following statements agree with the information given in the text on page 85?

In boxes 6–14 on your answer sheet, write

TRUE if the statement agrees with the information
FALSE if the statement contradicts the information
NOT GIVEN if there is no information on this

6   Builders have already started work on the new primary school.
7   The new school will take in children from outside Frog Valley.
8   There will be an increase in the number of shops.
9   The community centre will replace an existing social club building.
10 The swimming pool will be free for residents of Frog Valley.
11 The office space will accommodate businesses of different sizes.
12 The business car parking area will be underground.
13 The health centre will offer a wide range of new services.
14 At present, there are too few doctors at the health centre.

SECTION 2   Questions 15–27

Read the text below and answer Questions 15–24.

Percil Training Institute

Welcome to the Percil Training Institute. We hope that you will enjoy your course of training with us. This information is provided to introduce our Institute and to let you know some of the important features of our professional training courses.

Courses

Percil Training Institute was established to provide high quality short-duration training programmes for a range of professional needs. It has a highly trained and experienced teaching staff, many of whom have taught overseas.

Percil Training Institute provides courses in ten-week modules. Most courses (e.g. Office Management, Librarianship, Medical Records Organisation) consist of two modules, although some courses (Biotechnology, Computer Analysis) are three or four modules long. There is a break of two weeks between each module but since projects or assignments are set for completion in these periods, it is not possible to take vacations during this time.

Since each course has varying needs, there are not necessarily any set hours for classes across all programmes. You will need to consult the timetable for your course, which is printed at the front of your own course manual.

Please be reminded that Percil Training Institute cannot provide attendance or achievement certificates for students who have missed part of their course as a result of not reading their own course timetables properly. Legitimate reasons for non-attendance (e.g. illness) will be given consideration provided that documentary evidence is provided. In this case, an achievement certificate only will be issued.

Facilities

The opening times of the snack bar, coffee lounge and restaurant are printed below your course timetable. No bookings are required for any of the eating places except the restaurant for Friday and Saturday dinner. The coffee lounge and restaurant are not normally open on public holidays. However, a group booking may be made for the restaurant for dinner on such days, provided that there is a minimum of 20 people in the group. A non-refundable deposit will be required for such a booking.

The Institute has a very fine sports complex. The swimming pool is open daily from 8.00 am to 8.00 pm and can be used free of charge by all Percil students who present a valid student enrolment card. The squash courts can be booked by any student with a valid student card and the hire cost is $4.50 per half hour. The gymnasium is available for a ten-week membership fee of $40.00, or $5.00 per visit, or an annual subscription of $100. Guests of Percil students are welcome to use the swimming pool but not the gymnasium areas.

Security

Please be careful that you do not leave valuable items in the classroom areas at any time. Percil Training Institute cannot be held responsible for any loss or damage to students' property as a result of student negligence. After 8.30 pm the front doors of the Institute are locked. If you need to gain access to the Institute after this time, please contact the caretaker by pressing the doorbell and speaking through the intercom. If you are admitted by the caretaker you will be required to show your student card.

Medical Care

Minor accidents and injuries can usually be attended to on the premises, in the Health Centre on the third floor. These services are free. Headache pills and other analgesics are available at standard pharmacy prices.

Reading

Questions 15–24

Do the following statements agree with the information given in the text on pages 87 and 88?

In boxes 15–24 on your answer sheet, write

> **TRUE** *if the statement agrees with the information*
> **FALSE** *if the statement contradicts the information*
> **NOT GIVEN** *if there is no information on this*

15   All of the staff have overseas teaching experience.

16   All modules are of equal length.

17   Students are encouraged to take holidays in the two-week breaks between modules.

18   Courses may have very different timetables.

19   You can still obtain an attendance certificate if you have been absent through illness.

20   Permission is required for students to bring guests into the restaurant.

21   The coffee lounge is closed in the evenings.

22   Groups of 20 or more can make reservations to dine at the restaurant on public holidays.

23   Guests may use the swimming pool.

24   Students are unable to enter the institute after 8.30 pm.

Read the text below and answer Questions 25–27.

Percil Memorial Training Scholarships
(3 offered per year)

Percil Training Institute offers a number of scholarships for people from overseas who plan to live in Australia and need re-training. These scholarships are available for full-time study only and are not offered for courses of less than 20 weeks' duration.

Requirements/eligibility

Applicants for these scholarships must be of high academic ability as revealed in the qualifications they have already gained in their home country; alternatively, they must have at least five years of significant work experience in their chosen field and must produce evidence in the form of references from at least two employers or supervisors.

The award

These scholarships offer return airfares to Australia from your home country, provided that the distance by air from your city of departure to Sydney is not more than 2,500 kilometres. If the distance exceeds this amount, you will be provided with airline vouchers. Travel expenses to and from airports on both the outward and return journeys are paid for, and there is an airline excess baggage allowance of 120 kg.

Personal removal expenses for scholarship holders are not paid. If the scholarship holder is married at the time of applying for the scholarship, some travel and removal costs may be paid for the husband or wife. Travel costs or support for dependent children are at the scholarship holder's expense.

Scholars are eligible for assistance with accommodation within the Sydney metropolitan area, although married accommodation is unavailable on the Percil Institute campus. Since demand for accommodation on the campus is always high, scholarship applicants are advised to apply at least ten weeks before intending to come into residence.

Questions 25–27

Answer the questions below.

Choose **NO MORE THAN THREE WORDS AND/OR A NUMBER** from the text for each answer.

Write your answers in boxes 25–27 on your answer sheet.

25 To obtain a scholarship, what is the minimum course length?

26 What do scholarship winners receive towards their airfares if they live over 2,500 km from Sydney?

27 Who pays for dependent children to travel?

SECTION 3   Questions 28–40

Read the text below and answer Questions 28–40.

Divided opinions about letting farmland return to its natural state

Close to London's Gatwick Airport is Knepp Castle Estate, owned by Charlie Burrell. It is an intensive 3,500-acre farm that has been 'rewilded', that is, allowed to return to its natural, uncultivated state. After barely a decade, nature has come back astonishingly quickly. Neat fields of maize have been replaced with a landscape that resembles the typical grasslands of Africa. The original narrow clipped hedges that edged the farmland are now eight metres wide, and deer race through ragwort, thistles and other weeds in the meadows. The estate boasts more of the unusual purple emperor butterflies than anywhere else in Britain. It's also thought to be the only place where Britain's fastest-declining birds, turtle doves, are multiplying. But as rewilding blossoms, so do controversies.

In Wales, one ecologist says the concept can't even be mentioned to farmers. Even the harmless beaver is the subject of fierce debate: while it was recognised as a native animal in Scotland last year, beavers reintroduced in south-west England roam free only on a government trial. 'For us it is strange to see the British struggling with the beaver. Come on, we have thousands of them!' Dutch ecologist Leo Linnartz told a rewilding conference. Linnartz says that many Dutch objected to 'nature development' 30 years ago but rewilding principles are now mainstream.

In Britain, the rewilding movement started by writer and environmental activist George Monbiot is popularly seen to seek the return of large carnivores – bears, wolves and lynx. In practice, it is returning more modest herbivores like ponies and deer to the countryside. For decades, ecologists believed the end result of allowing a landscape to run wild would be dense forest and a mass extinction of sun-loving wild flowers and butterflies. But this belief has been demolished by Dutch ecologist Frans Vera. Since the 1980s, Vera has introduced wild cattle, horses and deer to rewilded marshland, and proved that 'natural' grazing creates a more dynamic landscape, a constantly changing pattern of open glades and wooded groves.

In the Scottish Highlands, rewilding is taking a different form as large landowners restore ancient pine forest. But David Balharry, former Scotland director of Rewilding Britain, cautions that rewilding in Scotland will only be championed by policymakers and politicians when it is led by local communities.

For Burrell, rewilding has been a pragmatic way to revive the struggling family farm. Ecotourism there makes as much profit as his conventional farm did. Knepp's unproductive soil meant Burrell could not compete with globalised food production. His profits may be steady while conventional dairy and cattle farm incomes fall dramatically, but no farmers have yet followed his example. 'It takes a new eye to look at this and say, "that's beautiful", rather than go, "that's just a real mess",' says Burrell. 'Other farmers may have a moral attitude towards it too – "why are you stopping food production?"' Many criticise rewilding for abandoning productive farmland when the world's population is growing.

Wouter Helmer, director of Rewilding Europe, sees no conflict between food production and rewilding: Europe is heading for a future of food produced more intensively in fewer areas, releasing less productive land for rewilding, he says. 'Farming is being done by fewer and fewer farmers on a larger scale on the best soils. They leave the less profitable lands to become adventure land for an increasingly urban population.'

Helmer says there is no point in seeking to feed the world with traditional organic farming because there is no one to do the labour: when he asks Dutch students who wants to farm, none raise their hands. 'They have a completely different relationship to nature to their parents or grandparents. They are not fighting with it on a daily basis. On one hand they are disconnected from nature but on the other hand they are becoming more relaxed with nature – it's hunting and gathering but hunting with a camera and gathering experiences. The part of the countryside which is not used for intensive farming starts to serve all these new urban needs.'

Yet some environmentalists worry how rewilding connects with urban populations. 'The challenge is how to make rewilding an issue that people in their ordinary lives can take action on,' says Elaine Gilligan of Friends of the Earth. She thinks it is great for engaging people in nature but doubts whether it is seen as important in large urban areas like Birmingham.

Rewilders argue that reducing flood risks for cities is one practical way rewilding can enhance urban life. Ted Green, founder president of the Ancient Tree Forum, believes that intensive farming can worsen flash flooding, and cause fertile earth to be swept downriver and out to sea. 'The land may belong to the landowner but the soil must belong to the nation,' says Green. 'When you see people cleaning out their houses after floods, you don't see them removing water, you see them removing mud. It's no longer an engineering problem – it's a farming problem.'

Some conservationists worry, however, that rewilding could replace the traditional protection of rare species on small nature reserves. 'If rewilding really takes off, there's a risk people will say, "Oh we don't have to do any of that old stuff,"' says Matt Shardlow, chief executive of Buglife. 'But we still have habitat fragmentation and species in tiny places and we have to take care of them even if you have some areas made bigger for wildlife.' Whatever happens, we need more projects like Knepp.

Test 4

Questions 28–30

Complete the summary below.

Choose **ONE WORD ONLY** from the text for each answer.

Write your answers in boxes 28–30 on your answer sheet.

Knepp Castle estate

About ten years ago, the decision was taken to rewild the farmland at Knepp Castle. Now the **28** .... that used to be grown there has disappeared and the countryside is more like parts of **29** .... The hedges surrounding the fields have been allowed to expand and deer can be seen running among the wild flowers. The estate hosts the largest number of **30** .... of a particular species in the whole country and bird numbers are increasing. All these changes have happened remarkably quickly.

Questions 31–36

Look at the following statements (Questions 31–36) and the list of people below.

*Match each statement with the correct person, **A–G**.*

*Write the correct letter, **A–G**, in boxes 31–36 on your answer sheet.*

31 Some people are against rewilding as it reduces the amount of crops that could provide much needed nourishment.

32 It may not be easy to get city residents to take part in rewilding.

33 Rewilding does not necessarily lead to a landscape thickly covered in trees.

34 It is acceptable to turn fields which do not yield many crops into natural spaces for people to enjoy.

35 The support of people living in the area is needed to make the authorities take rewilding seriously.

36 There is evidence that people get used to the idea of rewilding with time.

List of People
A Charlie Burrell
B Leo Linnartz
C George Monbiot
D Frans Vera
E David Balharry
F Wouter Helmer
G Elaine Gilligan

Test 4

Questions 37–40

Choose the correct letter, **A**, **B**, **C** or **D**.

Write the correct letter in boxes 37–40 on your answer sheet.

37 In the fifth paragraph, the writer points out that Burrell

    A had clear financial reasons for rewilding his farm.
    B is worried that his land now looks extremely untidy.
    C has considerably increased the money he makes from his farm.
    D was initially guided by other people who had let their land go wild.

38 What does Helmer say about young people and the land?

    A They want to leave it and find work in the city.
    B Many want to take over running their families' farms.
    C They have developed new ways of interacting with it.
    D Many are interested in building businesses on farmland.

39 Ted Green is particularly concerned that

    A there are increasing problems with water pollution in cities.
    B money needs to be invested to create more dams across rivers.
    C modern agricultural methods mean rain washes away productive soil.
    D more barriers are needed to prevent rivers flooding domestic homes.

40 In the final paragraph, what point is made about rewilding?

    A It will be very difficult to organise efficiently in large expanses of countryside.
    B It may attract so much public interest that smaller projects get forgotten.
    C It has caused problems for certain types of animals and insects in Britain.
    D It may be a trend that will lose its popularity quite quickly.

WRITING

WRITING TASK 1

You should spend about 20 minutes on this task.

> *You started in your present job two years ago. You now feel it is important for your career development to move to a different department in the same company.*
>
> *Write a letter to your manager. In your letter*
> - *say what you have learned in your present job*
> - *suggest how the company would benefit from moving you to a different department*
> - *explain why you do not wish to leave the company*

Write at least 150 words.

You do **NOT** need to write any addresses.

Begin your letter as follows:

Dear .... ,

Test 4

WRITING TASK 2

You should spend about 40 minutes on this task.

Write about the following topic:

> ***Nowadays famous people are photographed by professional photographers everywhere they go. Some people say this is a good thing because the public are interested in their lives. Other people think that photographers are wrong to follow famous people.***
>
> ***Discuss both these views and give your own opinion.***

Give reasons for your answer and include any relevant examples from your own knowledge or experience.

Write at least 250 words.

SPEAKING

PART 1

The examiner asks you about yourself, your home, work or studies and other familiar topics.

EXAMPLE

Cafés

- Do you have a favourite café? [Why/Why not?]
- Do you often go to cafés by yourself? [Why/Why not?]
- What do you think helps to make a café very popular? [Why?]
- Why do some people prefer cafés that are part of large chains, rather than small, local cafés?

PART 2

Describe a place you visited that has beautiful views.

You should say:
   where this place is
   when and why you visited it
   what views you can see from this place

and explain why you think these views are so beautiful.

You will have to talk about the topic for one to two minutes. You have one minute to think about what you are going to say. You can make some notes to help you if you wish.

PART 3

Discussion topics:

The beauty industry

Example questions:
Do you agree that most beauty products are a waste of money?
How does the beauty industry advertise its products so successfully?
What do you think of the view that beauty products should not be advertised to children?

Beauty and culture

Example questions:
Why do many people equate youth with beauty?
Do you think that being beautiful could affect a person's success in life?
Why might society's ideas about beauty change over time?

Audioscripts

TEST 1

PART 1

SALLY: Good morning. Hinchingbrooke Country Park, Sally speaking. I'm one of the rangers.

JOHN: Oh hello. My name's John Chapman, and I'm a teaching assistant at a local primary school. I've been asked to arrange a visit to the park for two of our classes.

SALLY: OK. What would you like to know?

JOHN: Well, I'm new to this area, so perhaps you could tell me something about the park first, please.

SALLY: Of course. Altogether the park covers 170 acres, that's <u>69</u> hectares. There are three main types of habitat: wetland, grassland and woodland. The woods are well established and varied, with an oak plantation, and other areas of mixed species. *Q1*

JOHN: Right.

SALLY: The wetland is quite varied, too. The original farmland was dug up around 40 years ago to extract gravel. Once this work was completed, the gravel pits filled with water, forming the two large lakes. There are also several smaller ones, ponds and a <u>stream</u> that flows through the park. *Q2*

JOHN: OK, so I suppose with these different habitats there's quite a variety of wildlife.

SALLY: There certainly is – a lot of different species of birds and insects, and also animals like deer and rabbits.

JOHN: And I understand you organise educational visits for school parties.

SALLY: That's right. We can organise a wide range of activities and adapt them to suit all ages.

JOHN: Can you give me some examples of the activities?

SALLY: Well, one focus is on science, where we help children to discover and study plants, trees and insects. They also collect and analyse <u>data</u> about the things they see. *Q3*

JOHN: Uhuh.

SALLY: Another focus is on geography. The park is a great environment to learn and practise reading a <u>map</u> and using a compass to navigate around the park. *Q4*

JOHN: Do you do anything connected with history?

SALLY: Yes, we do. For instance, the children can explore how the use of the land has changed over time. Then there's leisure and tourism.

JOHN: That focuses on your <u>visitors</u>, I would imagine. *Q5*

SALLY: Yes, mostly. The children find out about them, their requirements, the problems they may cause and how we manage these. And another subject we cover is music: here the children experiment with natural materials to create <u>sounds</u> and explore rhythm and tempo. *Q6*

JOHN: That must be fun!

SALLY: Most children really enjoy it.

SALLY: And of course, all the activities are educational, too. Learning outside the classroom encourages children to be creative, and to explore and discover for themselves.

JOHN:	I would imagine they get a sense of <u>freedom</u> that might not be a normal part of their lives.	*Q7*
SALLY:	That's right. And very often the children discover that they can do things they didn't know they could do, and they develop new <u>skills</u>. This gives them greater self-confidence.	*Q8*
JOHN:	It sounds great. So, what about the practical side of it? How much does it cost for a full-day visit? We would expect to bring between 30 and 40 children.	
SALLY:	If there are over 30, it costs £<u>4.95</u> for each child who attends on the day. We invoice you afterwards, so you don't pay for children who can't come because of sickness, for example. There's no charge for <u>leaders</u> and other adults – as many as you want to bring.	*Q9* *Q10*
JOHN:	That sounds very fair. Well, thanks for all the information. I'll need to discuss it with my colleagues, and I hope to get back to you soon to make a booking.	
SALLY:	We'll look forward to hearing from you. Goodbye.	
JOHN:	Goodbye, and thank you.	

PART 2

It's great to see so many members of the Twinning Association here tonight. Since the twinning link between our two towns, Stanthorpe here in England and Malatte in France, was established, the relationship between the towns has gone from strength to strength.

Last month, 25 members of the association from Stanthorpe spent a weekend in Malatte. Our hosts had arranged a great programme. We learned how cheese is produced in the region and had the chance to taste the products. The theme park trip had to be cancelled, but we all had a great time on <u>the final boat trip down the river – that was the real highlight</u>. *Q11*

This is a special year for the Association because it's 25 years since we were founded. In Malatte, they're planning to mark this by building a footbridge in the municipal park. We've been discussing what to do here and <u>we've decided to plant a poplar tree in the museum gardens</u>. We considered buying a garden seat to put there, but the authorities weren't happy with that idea. *Q12*

In terms of fundraising to support our activities, we've done very well. <u>Our pancake evening was well attended and made record profits</u>. And everyone enjoyed the demonstration of French cookery, which was nearly as successful. Numbers for our film show were limited because of the venue so we're looking for somewhere bigger next year. *Q13*

We're looking forward to welcoming our French visitors here next week, and I know that many of you here will be hosting individuals or families. The coach from France will arrive at 5 pm on Friday. Don't try to do too much that first evening as they'll be tired, so <u>have dinner in the house or garden rather than eating out</u>. The weather looks as if it'll be OK so you might like to plan a barbecue. Then the next morning's market day in town, and that's always a good place to stroll round. *Q14*

On Saturday evening, we'll all meet up at the football club, where once again <u>we'll have Toby Sharp and his band performing English and Scottish country songs</u>. Toby will already be well known to many of you as last year he organised our special quiz night and presented the prizes. *Q15*

Now on Sunday, we'll be taking our visitors to Farley House. You may not all be familiar with it, so here's a map to help you. You can see the car park at the bottom of the map. There's an excellent farm shop in the grounds where our visitors can buy local produce – <u>it's in the old stables, which is the first building you come to</u>. They're built round a courtyard, and the shop's <u>in the far corner on the left</u>. There's also a small café on the right as you go in. *Q16*

Audioscripts

I know that one or two of our visitors may not be all that mobile. The main entrance to the house has a lot of steps so you might want to use the disabled entry. <u>This is on the far side of the house from the car park</u>. Q17

Children will probably be most interested in the adventure playground. <u>That's at the northern end of the larger lake, in a bend on the path that leads to the lake</u>. There's lots for children to do there. Q18

There are a number of lovely gardens near the house. <u>The kitchen gardens are rectangular and surrounded by a wall. They're to the north-east of the house, quite near the smaller lake</u>. They're still in use and have a great collection of fruit and vegetables. Q19

The Temple of the Four Winds is a bit more of a walk – but it's worth it. Take the path from the car park and go past the western sides of the stables and the house. Then <u>when the path forks, take the right-hand path. Go up there with the woods on your left and the temple is right at the end</u>. There are great views over the whole area. Q20

OK, so that's . . .

PART 3

COLIN:	I haven't seen you for a bit, Marie.	
MARIE:	No. I've been busy with my project.	
COLIN:	You're making a vegan alternative to eggs, aren't you? Something that doesn't use animal products?	
MARIE:	Yes. I'm using chickpeas. I had two main aims when I first started looking for an alternative to eggs, but actually I've found chickpeas have got more advantages.	
COLIN:	Right.	
MARIE:	But how about *your* project on reusing waste food – you were looking at bread, weren't you?	
COLIN:	Yes. It's been hard work, but I've enjoyed it. The basic process was quite straightforward – breaking the stale bread down to a paste then reforming it.	
MARIE:	But you were using 3-D printing, weren't you, to make the paste into biscuits?	
COLIN:	Yeah, I'd used that before, but in this project, <u>I had time to play around with different patterns for the biscuits and finding how I could add fruit and vegetables to make them a more appetising colour, and I was really pleased with what I managed to produce</u>.	Q21/22
MARIE:	<u>It must've been a great feeling to make something appetising out of bits of old bread that would've been thrown away otherwise</u>.	Q21/22
COLIN:	<u>It was</u>. And I'm hoping that some of the restaurants in town will be interested in the biscuits. I'm going to send them some samples.	
MARIE:	I came across something on the internet yesterday that might interest you. It was a company that's developed touch-sensitive sensors for food labels.	
COLIN:	Mmm?	
MARIE:	It's a special sort of label on the food package. When the label's smooth, the food is fresh and then when you can feel bumps on the label, that means the food's gone bad. It started off as a project to help visually impaired people know whether food was fit to eat or not.	
COLIN:	Interesting. So just solid food?	
MARIE:	No, things like milk and juice as well. But actually, <u>I thought it might be really good for drug storage in hospitals and pharmacies</u>.	Q23/24
COLIN:	<u>Right</u>. And coming back to food, maybe it'd be possible to use it for other things besides freshness. Like <u>how many kilograms a joint of meat is, for example</u>.	Q23/24

102

MARIE:	Yes, there's all sorts of possibilities.	
COLIN:	I was reading an article about food trends predicting how eating habits might change in the next few years.	
MARIE:	Oh – things like more focus on local products? That seems so obvious, but the shops are still full of imported foods.	Q25
COLIN:	Yes, they need to be more proactive to address that.	
MARIE:	And somehow motivate consumers to change, yes.	
COLIN:	One thing everyone's aware of is the need for a reduction in unnecessary packaging – but just about everything you buy in supermarkets is still covered in plastic. The government needs to do something about it.	Q26
MARIE:	Absolutely. It's got to change.	
COLIN:	Do you think there'll be more interest in gluten- and lactose-free food?	
MARIE:	For people with allergies or food intolerances? I don't know. Lots of people I know have been buying that type of food for years now.	Q27
COLIN:	Yes, even if they haven't been diagnosed with an allergy.	
MARIE:	That's right. One thing I've noticed is the number of branded products related to celebrity chefs – people watch them cooking on TV and then buy things like spice mixes or frozen foods with the chef's name on . . . I bought something like that once, but I won't again.	Q28
COLIN:	Yeah – I bought a ready-made spice mix for chicken which was supposed to be used by a chef I'd seen on television, and it didn't actually taste of anything.	
MARIE:	Mm. Did the article mention 'ghost kitchens' used to produce takeaway food?	
COLIN:	No. What are they?	
MARIE:	Well, they might have the name of a restaurant, but actually they're a cooking facility just for delivery meals – the public don't ever go there. But people aren't aware of that – it's all kept very quiet.	Q29
COLIN:	So people don't realise the food's not actually from the restaurant?	
MARIE:	Right.	
COLIN:	Did you know more and more people are using all sorts of different mushrooms now, to treat different health concerns? Things like heart problems?	
MARIE:	Hmm. They might be taking a big risk there.	Q30
COLIN:	Yes, it's hard to know which varieties are safe to eat. Anyway maybe now . . .	

PART 4

For my presentation today, I'm going to talk about the Céide Fields in the northwest of Ireland, one of the largest Neolithic sites in the world. I recently visited this site and observed the work that is currently being done by a team of archaeologists there.

The site was first discovered in the 1930s by a local teacher, Patrick Caulfield. He noticed that when local people were digging in the bog, they were constantly hitting against what seemed to be rows of stones. He realised that these must be walls and that they must be thousands of years old for them to predate the bog which subsequently grew over them.   Q31

He wrote to the National Museum in Dublin to ask them to investigate, but no one took him seriously. It wasn't until 40 years later, when Patrick Caulfield's son Seamus, who had become an archaeologist by then, began to explore further. He inserted iron probes into the bog to map the formation of the stones, a traditional method which local people had always used for finding fuel buried in the bog for thousands of years. Carbon dating later proved that the site was over 5,000 years old and was the largest Neolithic site in Ireland.   Q32   Q33

103

Audioscripts

Thanks to the bog which covers the area, the remains of the settlement at Céide Fields, which is over 5,000 years old, are extremely well-preserved. A bog is 90 percent water; its soil is so saturated that when the grasses and heathers that grow on its surface die, they don't fully decay but accumulate in layers. <u>Objects remain so well preserved in these conditions because of the acidity of the peat and the deficiency of oxygen.</u> At least 175 days of rain a year are required for this to happen; this part of Ireland gets an average of 225 days.   Q34

The Neolithic farmers at Céide would have enjoyed several centuries of relative peace and stability. Neolithic farmers generally lived in larger communities than their predecessors, with a number of houses built around a community building. As they lived in permanent settlements, Neolithic farmers were able to build bigger <u>houses. These weren't round as people often assume, but rectangular</u> with a small hole in the roof that allowed smoke to escape. This is one of many innovations and indicates that the Neolithic farmers were the first people to cook indoors. Another new technology that Neolithic settlers brought to Ireland was pottery. Fragments of Neolithic pots have been found in Céide and elsewhere in Ireland. The pots were used for many things; as well as for storing food, pots were filled with a small amount of fat and when this was set alight, <u>they served as lamps</u>.   Q35 / Q36

It's thought that the Céide Fields were mainly used as paddocks for animals to graze in. Evidence from the Céide Fields suggests that <u>each plot of land was of a suitable size to sustain an extended family</u>. They may have used a system of rotational grazing in order to prevent over-grazing and to allow for plant recovery and regrowth. This must have been a year-round activity as <u>no structures have been found which would have been used to shelter animals in the winter</u>.   Q37 / Q38

However, archaeologists believe that this way of life at Céide ceased abruptly. Why was this? Well, several factors may have contributed to the changing circumstances. <u>The soil would have become less productive</u> and led to the abandonment of farming. The crop rotation system was partly responsible for this as it would have been very intensive and was not sustainable. But there were also climatic pressures too. The farmers at Céide would have enjoyed a relatively dry period, but this began to change and the conditions became wetter as <u>there was a lot more rain</u>. It was these conditions that encouraged the bog to form over the area which survives today.   Q39 / Q40

So now I'd like to show you some . . .

TEST 2

PART 1

WOMAN:	Hi Coleman, how are you?
COLEMAN:	Good, thanks.
WOMAN:	I wanted to have a chat with you because our friend Josh told me that you've joined a guitar group and it sounds interesting. I'd really like to learn myself.
COLEMAN:	Why don't you come along? I'm sure there's room for another person.
WOMAN:	Really? So – who runs the classes?
COLEMAN:	He's called a 'coordinator' – his name's Gary <u>Mathieson</u>. Q1
WOMAN:	Let me note that down. Gary. . . . How do you spell his surname?
COLEMAN:	It's M-A-T-H-I-E-S-O-N.
WOMAN:	Right, thanks.

104

COLEMAN:	He's retired, actually, but he's a really nice guy and he used to play in a lot of bands.	
WOMAN:	Thanks. So how long have you been going?	
COLEMAN:	About a month now.	
WOMAN:	And could you play anything before you started?	
COLEMAN:	I knew a few chords, but that's all.	
WOMAN:	I'm sure everyone will be better than me.	
COLEMAN:	That's what I thought, too. When I first spoke to Gary on the phone, he said it was a class for <u>beginners</u>, but I was still worried that everyone would be better than me, but we were all equally hopeless!	Q2
WOMAN:	Oh, that's reassuring. So where do you meet?	
COLEMAN:	Well, when I joined the group, they were meeting in Gary's home, but as the group got bigger, he decided to book a room at the <u>college</u> in town. I prefer going there.	Q3
WOMAN:	I know that place. I used to go to tap dancing classes there when I was at secondary school. I haven't been since, though and I can't remember what road it's in . . . is it Lock Street?	
COLEMAN:	It's just beyond there at the bottom of <u>New</u> Street near the city roundabout.	Q4
WOMAN:	Yes, of course.	
COLEMAN:	The guitar club is on the first floor in Room T347.	
WOMAN:	Right. And when do you meet? Is it at the weekend?	
COLEMAN:	We meet on Thursdays. It used to be 10.30 and that suited me well, but now we meet at <u>11</u>. The class that's in there before us asked if they could have the room for another 30 minutes.	Q5
WOMAN:	Oh, I see. Well, I'd love to come, but I don't have a guitar.	
COLEMAN:	Well, you can always buy a second-hand one. There's a website called 'The perfect <u>instrument</u>' that sells all kinds of guitars, violins and so on. I'm sure you'll find something there.	Q6

WOMAN:	So what's a typical lesson like with Gary?	
COLEMAN:	Well, he always starts by getting us to tune our guitars. That takes about five minutes.	
WOMAN:	Uhuh.	
COLEMAN:	Some people have an app they use, but others do it by <u>ear</u>. Gary goes round and helps them. And while he's doing that, he tells us what he's going to do during the lesson.	Q7
WOMAN:	Right.	
COLEMAN:	First, we usually spend about ten minutes doing some strumming.	
WOMAN:	So is that using . . . what are they called . . . plectrums?	
COLEMAN:	No – we just use our thumbs.	
WOMAN:	Much easier.	
COLEMAN:	Gary reminds us where to put our fingers for each chord and then we play them together. Sometimes we all just start laughing because we're so bad at keeping time, so Gary starts <u>clapping</u> to help us.	Q8
WOMAN:	Do you learn to play any songs?	
COLEMAN:	Yes – we do at least one song with words and chords. I mean that's harder than you think.	
WOMAN:	Oh, I'm sure it is!	
COLEMAN:	That part of the lesson takes about 15 minutes. He often brings a <u>recording</u> of the song and plays it to us first. Then he hands out the song and if there's a new chord in it, we practise that before we play it together – but really slowly.	Q9
WOMAN:	Do you do any finger picking?	

Audioscripts

COLEMAN:	That's the last ten minutes of the lesson, when we pick out the individual notes from a tune he's made up. It's always quite simple.
WOMAN:	That must be hard, though.
COLEMAN:	It is, but people like it because they can really concentrate and if we're all playing well, it sounds quite impressive. The only trouble is that he sometimes gets us to play one at a time – you know, <u>alone</u>.
WOMAN:	That's scary.
COLEMAN:	It is, but I've got used to it now. At the end he spends about five minutes telling us what to practise for the following week.
WOMAN:	Well, thanks Coleman. I'll go and have a look at that website, I think.

Q10

PART 2

H I never really planned to be a lifeboat volunteer when I came to live in Northsea. I'd been working in London as a website designer, but although that was interesting, I didn't like city life. <u>I'd been really keen on boats as a teenager, and I thought if I went to live by the sea, I might be able to pursue that interest a bit more in my free time</u>. Then I found that the Lifeboat Institution was looking for volunteers, so I decided to apply.

Q11

The Lifeboat Institution building here in Northsea's hard to miss, it's one of the largest in the country. It was built 15 years ago with <u>funds provided by a generous member of the public who'd lived here all her life</u>. As the Lifeboat Institution is a charity that relies on that kind of donation, rather than funding provided by the government, that was a huge help to us.

Q12

When I applied, I had to have a health assessment. The doctors were particularly interested in my vision. I used to be short-sighted, so I'd had to wear glasses, but I'd had laser eye surgery two years earlier so that was OK. <u>They gave me tests for colour blindness and they thought I might have a problem there</u>, but it turned out I was OK.

Q13

When the coastguard gets an alert, all the volunteers are contacted and rush to the lifeboat station. Our target's to get there in five minutes, then <u>we try to get the boat off the dock and out to sea in another six to eight minutes</u>. Our team's proud that we usually achieve that – the average time across the country's eight and a half minutes.

Q14

I've recently qualified as what's called a 'helmsman', which means I have the ultimate responsibility for the lifeboat. I have to check that the equipment we use is in working order – the crew have special life jackets that can support up to four people in the water. And <u>it's ultimately my decision whether it's safe to launch the boat</u>. But it's very rare not to launch it, even in the worst weather.

Q15

As well as going out on the lifeboat, my work involves other things too. A lot of people underestimate how quickly conditions can change at sea, so <u>I speak to youth groups and sailing clubs in the area about the sorts of problems that sailors and swimmers can have</u> if the weather suddenly gets bad. We also have a lot of volunteers who organise activities to raise money for us, and we couldn't manage without them.

Q16

The training we get is a continuous process, focusing on technical competence and safe handling techniques, and <u>it's given me the confidence to deal with extreme situations without panicking</u>. I was glad I'd done a first aid course before I started, as that's a big help with the casualty care activities we do. We've done a lot on how to deal with ropes and tie knots – that's an essential skill. After a year, I did a one-week residential course, led by specialists. They had a wave-tank where they could create extreme weather conditions – so <u>we could get experience at what to do if the boat turned over in a storm at night, for example</u>.

Q17/18

Q17/18

Since I started, I've had to deal with a range of emergency situations.

But the work's hugely motivating. It's not just about saving lives – I've learned a lot about the technology involved. My background in IT's been useful here, and I can use my expertise to help other volunteers. <u>They're a great group – we're like a family really</u>, which helps when you're dragging yourself out of bed on a cold stormy night. But actually, <u>it's the colder months that can be the most rewarding time</u>. That's when the incidents tend to be more serious, and you realise that you can make a huge difference to the outcome.

Q19/20

So if any of you listeners are interested. . . .

PART 3

BELLA:	Hi Don – did you get the copy of the article on recycling footwear that I emailed you?
DON:	Yeah – it's here . . . I've had a look at it.
BELLA:	So do you think it's a good topic for our presentation?
DON:	Well, before I started reading it, I thought *recycling footwear*, well, although it's quite interesting, <u>perhaps there isn't enough to say about it</u>, cos we put shoes in recycling bins, they go to charity shops and that's about it.
BELLA:	. . . but there's much more to it than that.
DON:	I realise that now and I'm keen to research the topic more.
BELLA:	That's great.
DON:	One of the things I didn't realise until I read the article was just how many pairs of trainers get recycled!
BELLA:	Well, a lot of young people wear them all the time now. They've become more popular than ordinary shoes.
DON:	I know. I guess they *are* very hard-wearing, but <u>don't they look a bit casual for school uniform? I don't think they're right for that</u>.
BELLA:	<u>Actually, I think some of them look quite smart on pupils</u> . . . better than a scruffy old pair of shoes. So do you keep shoes a *long* time?
DON:	Yes. Though I do tend to wear my old pairs for doing dirty jobs like cleaning my bike.
BELLA:	I must admit, I've <u>recycled some perfectly good shoes, that haven't gone out of fashion and still fit, just because they don't look great on me any more</u>. That's awful isn't it?
DON:	I think it's common because there's so much choice. The article did say that recent sales of footwear have increased enormously.
BELLA:	That didn't surprise me.
DON:	No. But then it said that <u>the amount of recycled footwear has fallen: it's 6 percent now compared to a previous level of 11 percent. That doesn't seem to make sense.</u>
BELLA:	That's because not everything goes through the recycling process. Some footwear just isn't good enough to re-sell, for one reason or another, and gets rejected.

Q21

Q22

Q23

Q24

BELLA:	So let's find some examples in the article of footwear that was rejected for recycling.
DON:	OK. I think there are some in the interview with the recycling manager. Yeah – here it is.
BELLA:	Mmm. Let's start with the ladies' high-heeled shoes. What did he say about those?
DON:	He said they were probably expensive – the material was suede and they were beige in colour – it looked like someone had only worn them once, *but* in a very wet field so <u>the heels were too stained with mud and grass to re-sell them</u>.

Q25

Audioscripts

BELLA:	OK . . . and the leather ankle boots. What was wrong with them?
DON:	Apparently, the heels were worn – but that wasn't the problem. <u>One of the shoes was a much lighter shade than the other one</u> – it had obviously been left in the sun. I suppose even second-hand shoes should look the same!
BELLA:	Sure. Then there were the red baby shoes.
DON:	Oh yes – we're told to tie shoes together when we put them in a recycling bin, but people often don't bother.
BELLA:	<u>You'd think it would have been easy to find the other, but it wasn't</u>. That was a shame because they were obviously new.
DON:	The trainers were interesting. He said they looked like they'd been worn by a marathon runner.
BELLA:	Yeah – weren't they split?
DON:	Not exactly. <u>One of the soles was so worn under the foot that you could put your finger through it</u>. Well, we could certainly use some of those examples in our presentation to explain why 90 percent of shoes that people take to recycling centres or bins get thrown into landfill.
BELLA:	Mmm. What did you think about the project his team set up to avoid this by making new shoes out of the *good* parts of old shoes?
DON:	It sounded like a good idea. They get so many shoes, they should be able to match parts. I wasn't surprised that it failed, though. I mean who wants to buy second-hand shoes really? Think of all the germs you could catch!
BELLA:	Well, people didn't refuse them for that reason, did they? <u>It was because the pairs of shoes weren't identical</u>.
DON:	They still managed to ship them overseas, though.
BELLA:	That's another area we need to discuss.
DON:	You know I used to consider this topic just from my own perspective, by thinking about my own recycling behaviour without looking at the bigger picture. So much happens once shoes leave the recycling area.
BELLA:	It's not as simple as you first think, and <u>we can show that by taking a very different approach to it</u>.
DON:	Absolutely. So let's discuss . . .

Q26

Q27

Q28

Q29

Q30

PART 4

For my project on invertebrates, I chose to study tardigrades. These are microscopic – or to be more precise – near-microscopic animals. There are well over a thousand known species of these tiny animals, which belong to the phylum *Tardigrada*. Most tardigrades range in length from 0.05 to 1 millimetre, though the largest species can grow to be 1.2 millimetres in length. They are also sometimes called 'water bears': 'water' because that's where they thrive best, and 'bear' <u>because of the way they move</u>. 'Moss piglet' is another name for tardigrades because of the way they look when viewed from the front. They were first discovered in Germany in 1773 by Johann Goeze, who coined the name *Tardigrada*.

Q31

As I say, there are many different species of tardigrade – too many to describe here – but, generally speaking, the different species share similar physical traits. <u>They have a body which is short</u>, and also rounded – a bit like a barrel – and the body comprises four segments. Each segment has a pair of legs, at the end of which are between four and eight sharp claws. I should also say that some species don't have any claws; <u>what they have are discs</u>, and these work by means of suction. They enable the tardigrade to cling on to surfaces or to grip its prey. Within the body, there are no lungs, or any organs for breathing at all. Instead, <u>oxygen and also blood are transported in a fluid that fills the cavity of the body</u>.

Q32

Q33

Q34

As far as the tardigrade's head is concerned, the best way I can describe this is that it looks rather strange – a bit squashed even – though many of the websites I looked at described its appearance as cute, which isn't exactly very scientific. The tardigrade's mouth is a kind of tube that can open outwards to reveal teeth-like structures known as 'stylets'. These are sharp enough to pierce plant or animal cells. *Q35*

So, where are tardigrades found? Well, they live in every part of the world, in a variety of habitats: most commonly, on the bed of a lake, or on many kinds of plants or in very wet environments. There's been some interesting research which has found that tardigrades are capable of surviving radiation and very high pressure, and they're also able to withstand temperatures as cold as –200 degrees centigrade, or highs of more than 148 degrees centigrade, which is incredibly hot. *Q36*

It has been said that tardigrades could survive long after human beings have been wiped out, even in the event of an asteroid hitting the earth. If conditions become too extreme and tardigrades are at risk of drying out, they enter a state called cryptobiosis. They curl into a ball, called a tun – that's T-U-N – by retracting their head and legs, and their metabolism drops to less than one percent of normal levels. They can remain like this until they are re-introduced to water, when they will come back to life in a matter of a few hours. While in a state of cryptobiosis, tardigrades produce a protein that protects their DNA. In 2016, scientists revived two tardigrades that had been tuns for more than 30 years. There was a report that, in 1948, a 120-year-old tun was revived, but this experiment has never been repeated. There are currently several tests taking place in space, to determine how long tardigrades might be able to survive there. I believe the record so far is 10 days. *Q37* *Q38*

So, erm, moving on. In terms of their diet, tardigrades consume liquids in order to survive. Although they have teeth, they don't use these for chewing. They suck the juices from moss, or extract fluid from seaweed, but some species prey on other tardigrades, from other species or within their own. I suppose this isn't surprising, given that tardigrades are mainly comprised of liquid and are coated with a type of gel. *Q39*

Finally, I'd like to mention the conservation status of tardigrades. It is estimated that they have been in existence for approximately half a billion years and, in that time, they have survived five mass extinctions. So, it will probably come as no surprise to you, that tardigrades have not been evaluated by the International Union for Conservation of Nature and are not on any endangered list. Some researchers have described them as thriving. *Q40*

Does anyone have any questions they'd like to ask?

TEST 3

PART 1

LEON:	Hi Shannon – how are you settling into your new flat?
SHANNON:	Really well, thanks.
LEON:	You look like you're going shopping.
SHANNON:	Yes, I am. My cousins are coming to stay for a couple of days, and I have to cook for them.
LEON:	Well, there are plenty of places to buy food in Kite Place – it's the area by the harbour.
SHANNON:	Oh, OK, I'll find that on the map. Thanks.
LEON:	What sort of food do you need to get?
SHANNON:	Well, neither of them eats meat but they both like fish.

Q1

Audioscripts

LEON:	Well, there's a really good fish market there.	
SHANNON:	Oh great – where is it exactly?	
LEON:	It's at the far end of Kite Place, so you have to go over the <u>bridge</u> and then it's on the right.	Q2
SHANNON:	OK – is it open all day?	
LEON:	It doesn't close until four, but I'd recommend going earlier than that – it does run out of some things.	
SHANNON:	Oh, I don't want that to happen.	
LEON:	As long as you get there by <u>3.30</u>, you should be fine. It's only 11 now, so plenty of time.	Q3
SHANNON:	Right.	
LEON:	Do you need to buy vegetables too?	
SHANNON:	I do, and I want to avoid all the plastic packaging in the supermarket!	
LEON:	Well, there's a really nice organic shop there. Now what's it called . . . it's the name of a flower. I know, it's '<u>Rose</u>'.	Q4
SHANNON:	That's a nice name.	
LEON:	Yeah – it sells vegetables and quite a lot of other stuff.	
SHANNON:	And where's that?	
LEON:	Well, as you reach the market, you'll see a big grey building on your left – I think it used to be a warehouse. Anyway, now it's a restaurant upstairs, but the ground floor has two shops either side of the entrance and it's the one on the left.	
SHANNON:	That's easy enough.	
LEON:	You can't miss it – there's also a big <u>sign</u> on the pavement so you can look for that.	Q5
SHANNON:	Fine! I guess if I need anything else, I'll have to go to the supermarket.	
LEON:	Yeah – you should be able to get everything you need, but there's a minibus that goes to the supermarket if you need it. It's <u>purple</u> and the number is 289.	Q6
SHANNON:	Thanks, that's great.	

LEON:	So what do you need to get at the fish market? The salmon is always very good and the shellfish.	
SHANNON:	I'm going to make a curry, I think, and I need about 12 prawns for that.	
LEON:	They'll have plenty of those.	
SHANNON:	OK.	
LEON:	Have you ever tried <u>samphire</u>?	Q7
SHANNON:	No – what's that?	
LEON:	It's a type of seaweed. I just ask for a handful and you fry it in butter. It's delicious!	
SHANNON:	Oh, I might try that – how do you spell it?	
LEON:	It's S-A-M-P-H-I-R-E.	
SHANNON:	Great – it's always good to try something different.	
LEON:	Yeah.	
SHANNON:	I'll see what beans they have in the organic shop and I think I'll get something for dessert there.	
LEON:	How about a mango?	
SHANNON:	I'm not sure – they're not always ripe. I'd prefer a <u>melon</u> – it's bigger too.	Q8
LEON:	Good idea. The owner also sells a lot of spices there that you can put in a curry, and things like <u>coconut</u>.	Q9
SHANNON:	Oh, that's very helpful. I'll have a look.	
LEON:	No problem.	
SHANNON:	I know bread doesn't really go with curry but I always like to have some in case.	
LEON:	As I said – all the bread is home-made and there's lots of variety. I like the brown bread myself.	
SHANNON:	Mm, sounds good.	

LEON:	They sell other things there too.	
SHANNON:	Like cakes? I love chocolate cake.	
LEON:	Well – not that, but they have a whole range of tarts and the best are the <u>strawberry</u> ones.	Q10
SHANNON:	Perfect – hopefully I won't even have to go to the supermarket!	

PART 2

PRESENTER:	The children's book festival is coming up again soon and here to tell us all about it is the festival's organiser, Jenny Morgan. So tell us what we can expect this year, Jenny.	
JENNY:	Well, as usual we've got five days of action-packed exciting events for children, with writers coming from all over the country getting involved.	
	Just to give you an idea of what's on offer in the workshops, first of all, there's a very special event called Superheroes. <u>This is a chance for deaf children to share their reading experiences</u> with author Madeleine Gordon, who is herself hearing impaired.	Q11
	'Just do it' is a practical workshop led by the well-known illustrator Mark Keane. He'll take participants on a magical journey to faraway lands with <u>an opportunity for aspiring actors to do some role play</u>.	Q12
	'Count on me' is an inspiring and entertaining look at the issues of friendship <u>for 13–14-year-olds</u>. It looks at some of the friendships described in popular books and asks participants to compare these with their own experiences.	Q13
	'Speak up' is part of a series of workshops on the subject of mental health. This is a creative writing workshop <u>encouraging children to describe situations where young people experience loneliness</u>. A recent survey revealed that children can be lonely even when they're at home with their families.	Q14
	'Jump for joy', as many of you will know, is the heart-warming, best-selling story by Nina Karan about a young girl's trip to visit her relatives in India. <u>It recently received the gold medal at the Waterford Awards. Nina will get children to celebrate</u> the word 'joy' by writing a poem.	Q15
	'Sticks and stones' is the beautifully illustrated picture book for young readers about a community who organise an African-Caribbean festival <u>to help local children learn about their Jamaican roots</u>. This will be a musical event where children will have the chance to play steel drums. This is bound to be very popular, so please book as soon as possible.	Q16

PRESENTER:	Thanks Jenny. That all sounds really interesting. I'm just wondering if you have a favourite book you could recommend for our readers?	
JENNY:	It's hard to choose, but *Alive and Kicking* is definitely worth mentioning. You won't have heard of the writer as it's her first book – which is really impressive. It's basically the teenage diary of a boy from Somalia who comes to live in the UK. <u>It deals with the serious issue of immigration</u> and all the challenges the boy has to face at school and with the language barrier, etc. Usually, books like this are quite sad, but <u>this one actually made me cry with laughter</u>. On each page, there are simple but hilarious black and white stick drawings of the boy with his friends and teachers. At the end of each diary entry, there are new English words the boy learns each day, which may help develop some children's vocabulary.	Q17/18 Q17/18
PRESENTER:	I think my kids would enjoy that. What about any advice for parents on how to encourage their children to read more?	

Audioscripts

JENNY: Well, this is something I get asked about a lot. There are so many distractions for kids these days that it can be hard to find time for reading. One thing I'd say is to make time to sit down with your child and share books with them. A lot of parents give up reading aloud to their children as soon as they learn to read independently, but this is a mistake. It's good to read more advanced books to them as it helps to develop their vocabulary. If you don't have time for this, then let them listen to audio books. Often, they'll want to read books they've listened to for themselves. I think it's a good idea to make a mental note of the type of books your child is reading – often they just read the same genre all the time, which can get a bit boring. You can introduce new authors and genres to them. Librarians should be able to help you with this.   Q19/20

PRESENTER: Well Jenny, I think that's really useful. . . .

PART 3

CLARE: Hi Jake. How are you getting on with the practical teaching?
JAKE: It's harder than I expected, but I've got some great classes. How about you?
CLARE: Not brilliant. I'm really struggling with my Year 12 science class.
JAKE: Are they hard to control?
CLARE: Well, I don't have discipline problems as such. It's just that they don't seem to think that science has anything to do with their lives. It's depressing. They listen to what I say, and I gave them a test last week and the results weren't too bad, but there's no real engagement.   Q21
JAKE: Right.
CLARE: And as part of my teaching practice, I have to design an experiment for them to do. I was wondering about something on the children's diets . . . you know, asking them to record what they eat and maybe linking it to their state of health.
JAKE: Mmm. Let's think. So your methodology would involve the children recording what they eat. OK, but you'd also need to have access to the children's medical records and I don't think people would be happy about that; confidentiality would be an issue. If you could get the right data, the conclusions might be significant, but I suspect it's not going to be easy.   Q22
CLARE: Right.
JAKE: Have you thought about doing an experiment using animals?
CLARE: Wouldn't that be upsetting for the children?
JAKE: Well, the animals don't have to be harmed in any way. It could just be an experiment where they're given a certain diet and the effects are observed.
CLARE: Would I have to get permission to use animals?
JAKE: Yes, you'd have to submit an outline of the experiment and fill in a form, but it's quite straightforward.
CLARE: But if we found out that, say, a particular diet affects the health of animals, the same thing wouldn't necessarily be true for people, would it?   Q23
JAKE: No that's true, but the findings for any experiment are going to be limited. It's inevitable.
CLARE: I suppose so. So what animals could I use to investigate the effects of diet? Mice?
JAKE: Yes. You'd need experimental mice – ones that have been specially bred for experiments.
OK, so what will your experiment be investigating exactly?
CLARE: Well, something to do with nutrition. So maybe we could look at food supplements . . . things like extra iron and extra protein, and their impact on health.

JAKE:	Mmm. That might be rather broad. Maybe just look at the effects of one supplement, like sugar, on the health of the mice?	
CLARE:	In fact, maybe the focus could be on whether mice can control their own diet. . . .	Q24
JAKE:	So, what happens when they have access to more sugar, that they don't really need?	
CLARE:	Exactly. Do they eat it or do they decide to leave it?	
JAKE:	Great. Then later on, you could do a follow-up experiment adding another variable. Like, you could give some of the mice the chance to be more active, running on a wheel or something, and the others just sit around and don't do much.	Q25
CLARE:	Or I could repeat the experiment but change the type of food I provided . . . or use mice with a different genetic structure. But I think your idea would be more interesting, I might think about that some more.	

CLARE:	So can I talk through a possible procedure for the experiment where mice are given a sugar supplement?	
JAKE:	Sure. I did a similar experiment in college actually.	
CLARE:	Great. So how many mice would I need?	
JAKE:	I'd say about 12. And all young ones, not a mixture of old and young.	Q26
CLARE:	OK. And I'd need two groups of equal sizes, so six in each group. And how would I tell them apart? I suppose I could put some sort of tag on one group . . . or just mark them in some way?	Q27
JAKE:	You could use food colouring, that wouldn't hurt them.	
CLARE:	Perfect. Then each group would go into a separate cage, and one group, let's call them group A, would be the control group. So they'd just have ordinary mouse food. I suppose you can buy that?	
JAKE:	Yes, it comes in dry pellets.	
CLARE:	And the other group would have the same as the first group, but they'd also have the extra sugar.	
JAKE:	Would you just give them straight sugar?	
CLARE:	It might be better to give them something like cereal with it.	Q28
JAKE:	Mmm. Then you'd need to weigh the mice, I should think once a week. And you'd need an electronic balance.	
CLARE:	But we can't hold them on the balance, or it'd affect the reading.	
JAKE:	Exactly. So you need something called a weighing chamber to stop the mice from running away. It sounds complicated, but actually you can just use a plastic box with holes in the top.	Q29
CLARE:	OK. So once we've measured the weight gain of each mouse we can work out the average for each group, as well as the standard deviation. And then see where we go from there. That sounds cool, I think the students will enjoy it.	Q30
JAKE:	Yes. One thing . . .	

PART 4

In today's lecture, I'm going to be talking about microplastics.

Microplastics are tiny pieces of plastic smaller than five millimetres in size. Recently there's been a greater awareness that there are large quantities of plastic waste – big and small – in the environment. The amount of plastic waste in the oceans has received widespread attention, but far less is known about the effects of microplastics in freshwater and particularly in soil.

Microplastics can enter the environment via a number of different sources. Threads and microfibres detach from synthetic clothing every time they're put in a washing machine, and   Q31

Audioscripts

these find their way into the water system. Other sources include big pieces of plastic waste that are already in the environment, and these break down into microscopic particles over a period of time. On a larger scale, factory waste is another route, as are tyres which wear down as cars, lorries and so on travel along road surfaces.

We already understand some of the impacts of microplastics from studies involving fish and other animals. There is evidence that microplastics harm small creatures in a variety of ways, such as by <u>damaging their mouths</u>, or by impairing their ability to feed, for example when microplastics get lodged in their digestive system.   *Q32*

Surprisingly perhaps, it is likely that humans consume microplastics, as these have been detected in a wide range of food and drink products, including bottled water, as well as in water that comes direct from the tap. What's more, <u>salt and many kinds of seafood have also been found to contain microplastics</u>.   *Q33*

However, it's important to underline that there is not yet conclusive proof that microplastics cause significant harm to people. In many countries, including here in the UK, there is <u>legislation which prevents manufacturers from adding plastic microbeads to shower gels, facial cleansers and toothpaste</u>.   *Q34*

It is very difficult to accurately estimate the total amount of microplastic particles in the soil as they can be hard to detect, but we do know they are carried in the air and deposited in the soil by rain. What's more, <u>many of the fertilisers used by both farmers and gardeners contain microplastics</u>.   *Q35*

A team from the Anglia Ruskin University in Cambridge has carried out a study of the effects of microplastics on the digestive tracts of earthworms. These worms, which live in topsoil, are an essential component of our agricultural system. <u>By feeding on soil, they mix nutrients into it, thereby making it more fertile</u>.   *Q36*

The researchers set out to discover whether the introduction of microplastics into the soil – and the subsequent <u>ingestion of these by earthworms – would impact soil quality and ultimately inhibit plant growth</u>. The short answer was, yes, it did. After placing three different types of microplastic particles into the soil, they planted perennial rye grass. The particles of microplastic, which included biodegradable PLA and conventional high-density polyethylene, or HDPE, were then ingested by the earthworms in the soil. <u>The result was that the worms lost weight rapidly</u>. What's more, a lower percentage than normal of the rye grass seeds germinated, and the researchers concluded that this was a direct result of the earthworms being unable to fulfil their normal role in making soil more fertile. The team also discovered that <u>there was an increase in the amount of acid found in the soil</u>, and this was attributed mainly to the microplastic particles from conventional HDPE plastic.   *Q37*   *Q38*   *Q39*

The conclusions of the study make for very interesting reading – I've included the reference in the notes to give you at the end of this session. To summarise, the authors proposed the idea that we need to regard soil as we would regard any other process in nature. This means we should accept the implications of soil being dependent on decaying and dead matter constantly being passed through the bodies of earthworms. That is, when soil becomes impoverished by the presence of microplastics, <u>not only ecosystems but also the whole of society are negatively impacted</u>.   *Q40*

TEST 4

PART 1

KAEDEN: Hello Charlotte. I'm Kaeden, one of the supervisors. Welcome to the team.
CHARLOTTE: Hi Aiden.
KAEDEN: It's <u>Kaeden</u>.   Q1
CHARLOTTE: I'm so sorry.
KAEDEN: Don't worry. People often get my name wrong; they never know how to spell it. It's K-A-E-D-E-N, in case you ever need to write it.
CHARLOTTE: I'll try and remember.
KAEDEN: So, there are a few practical things you need to sort out this morning. Then I'll show you what you're going to do today.
CHARLOTTE: The email I received said to go to the front desk, to show my letter of appointment and pick up my badge.
KAEDEN: You'll need that for the staffroom and other areas of the supermarket where shoppers aren't allowed.
So, after you've finished at the front desk, I'll take you to the staffroom. Put your coat and rucksack in one of the <u>lockers</u> there. Take whichever one is free.   Q2
CHARLOTTE: Will I have a key?
KAEDEN: Yes. Try not to lose it. At the end of the day, leave it in the door for the next person to use.
CHARLOTTE: Will do.
KAEDEN: You also need to go to the HR department to see Tiffany. She's really helpful.
CHARLOTTE: I was told to bring my <u>passport</u> with me. HR need to take a note of the number in it.   Q3
KAEDEN: That's right. Or you can show your ID card.
CHARLOTTE: I don't have one of those.
KAEDEN: OK. Tiffany will give you a <u>uniform</u>. They have lots in different sizes, so you just tell her what you need. I won't come with you to HR – I've got to go and sort something else out. Problem with a bread slicer.   Q4
CHARLOTTE: Is the HR office near the staffroom?
KAEDEN: The staffroom's on the first floor, and HR are a couple of floors above that, on the <u>third</u> floor. There's a staircase outside the staffroom.   Q5
CHARLOTTE: OK.
KAEDEN: When you've finished with HR, come and find me in the bakery section of the shop.
CHARLOTTE: I'm looking forward to getting started.
KAEDEN: I'll just give you my phone number, in case you can't find me. Have you got your phone there?
CHARLOTTE: Yes . . . OK, ready.
KAEDEN: It's <u>oh-four-one-two double-six-five nine-oh-three</u>.   Q6
CHARLOTTE: OK, done.

KAEDEN: So, Charlotte, your tasks today are in the bakery section, on the sushi counter, and on the meat and fish counters. The first job is to check sell-by dates on the bread and cakes. If any of the dates are today's, put a new price label on the packaging.
CHARLOTTE: What if any of the labels are yesterday's dates, or older? Do I throw those items away?

115

Audioscripts

KAEDEN: Yes, but that shouldn't happen – we check the stock every day. When something needs a new price label, put a <u>yellow</u> one on the package, next to the original price.   Q7
CHARLOTTE: OK.
KAEDEN: After that, you'll go to the sushi takeaway counter.
CHARLOTTE: Will I be preparing boxes of food?
KAEDEN: For today, you'll just be helping the staff.
CHARLOTTE: Yes, of course.
KAEDEN: You'll see lots of flat cardboard boxes at one end of the counter. Beneath those is where we keep the <u>plastic</u> boxes – we run out of those really quickly, so you should bring more from the storeroom.   Q8
CHARLOTTE: Is that my only task on the sushi counter?
KAEDEN: No. You also need to clean the area where they prepare the dishes. There are cloths and bottles of spray by the sink. Oh, and please make sure you clean *that* too.
CHARLOTTE: Sure. That's important, isn't it?
KAEDEN: Absolutely. But you mustn't wash up knives. You have to do some training before you're allowed to touch sharp objects.
CHARLOTTE: What should I do if there are any?
KAEDEN: Ask someone to put them in the dishwasher.
CHARLOTTE: OK, thanks. I don't want to get anything wrong.
KAEDEN: Don't worry. You'll be fine. And I'll be around to help.
CHARLOTTE: Right.
KAEDEN: Finally, the meat and fish counters. You need to clean the area where staff serve customers, including wiping the weighing scales.
CHARLOTTE: OK. Anything else?
KAEDEN: The fish is laid on <u>ice</u>, but when that starts to melt, you'll need to get more from the cold-room.   Q9
CHARLOTTE: I know the staff on the food counters wear a hat. Will that be the same for me?
KAEDEN: You won't be serving customers directly, so no. But make sure you put on thermal <u>gloves</u> when you take anything out of the cold-room. The temperature's low enough in there to get frostbite from touching things.   Q10
CHARLOTTE: Understood.

PART 2

My name's Liz Fuller and I'm a running coach with Compton Park Runners Club.

Welcome to my podcast. If you're thinking about taking up running – I'm here to help.

There are many training programmes available online which aim to help people build up to running 5 kilometres. Some of them are great and thousands of people of all ages are taking part in 5-kilometre races across the country as a result. People like them because they're easy to follow and don't push them too hard. However, <u>they don't work for everyone – especially if you suffer from something like a heart condition or asthma</u>, because they're aimed at people with average fitness and running ability. Another thing is that everyone is different – and <u>if you have any specific questions related to your needs, there's no one to provide any answers</u>.   Q11/12 Q11/12

I have a couple of simple tips I always give to new runners. I expect you've been told to run very slowly until your fitness increases – well, I find that can prevent progress. You should run at a speed that feels comfortable, but time yourself and try to run a bit faster each time. <u>Listening to music can be very helpful – it takes your mind off things and helps your body get into a rhythm</u>. I'd say that is better than running with a friend – especially as most people are   Q13/14 competitive and that's not what you want when you're just starting. I don't think the time of day is especially important – some people are better in the evening, while others are morning people – but you need to be consistent, so <u>aim to train regularly – twice a week is enough to begin with</u>. *Q13/14*

New members often say to me that they've been put off running either because they lack confidence, or they don't have time, or they think they dislike running. Ceri, for example, joined the club two years ago at the age of 40. She'd always enjoyed running at school but <u>wasn't sure if she'd be able to do it. She was worried about being left behind and being the slowest runner</u>. But she says she was made to feel so welcome she soon forgot all about that. *Q15*

<u>James had always hated the idea of running</u> but a friend encouraged him to come along for a taster session and he hasn't looked back. He never misses a training session despite having a really demanding job. *Q16*

Leo was worried about having to commit himself to training sessions every week and <u>wasn't sure he'd be able to fit training into his busy schedule</u>. But after experiencing a lot of stress at work he came along to us and gave it a go. Now he says he feels much more relaxed and he looks forward to his weekly run. *Q17*

Mark is quite typical of our new members. He's never considered himself to be a sporty person and it was only when he retired that he decided to take up the challenge of trying to run 5 kilometres. <u>It took him months to find the courage to contact us</u> but he felt reassured immediately as there were other people his age who were only just taking up running for the first time. *Q18*

My own journey hasn't been easy. I did my first marathon when I was 37, after having had two kids. My husband had been running marathons for years, but I never dreamed I'd be doing one with him. I managed to complete it in four hours, but <u>I felt like giving up halfway through – it was only the support of the spectators that kept me going</u>. *Q19*

I do think signing up for a race of whatever length is motivating – whether it's 5K or 25K – because it's good to have something to work towards and it gives you a sense of achievement. I did my first 10K after only six months, which was certainly very challenging and not something I'd necessarily recommend. But <u>after you've been training for a few weeks, it's worth putting your name down for a 5K</u> – some people find they only need a few practice runs before taking part in a race, but I'd give yourself a couple of months at least. *Q20*

Well, I hope that's given . . .

PART 3

KIERAN: So Jane – you'll be off to Denmark soon to do your work placement.
JANE: Yes, I'm really looking forward to it and I've just started packing up all my books to put in storage.
KIERAN: Well, I hope they don't get spoilt.
JANE: It's OK – my grandfather works in a bookshop and he told me how to pack them.
KIERAN: Oh, that's helpful.
JANE: He says <u>you have to support the spine otherwise the paper can come away from the cover</u>. *Q21*
KIERAN: <u>Yeah – that's obvious</u>.
JANE: <u>He also told me to pack them flat in the box not on their side – again because they can bend and if you leave them like that for, say, a year, it's quite hard to get them back to their normal shape</u>.

Audioscripts

KIERAN:	Well, it's pretty clear that ruins them, but a lot of people just can't be bothered to protect their books.
JANE:	He always says it's such a shame that publishers don't use better-quality paper.
KIERAN:	It's the acid in the paper that causes the problem, isn't it?
JANE:	Yeah – that's why old books go yellow. You know some of the books my grandfather's given me are like that already.
KIERAN:	Oh . . .
JANE:	I should dump them really if they're going to deteriorate further, but I'd feel bad. They'll always remind me of him. He's quite a collector, you know.
KIERAN:	Well, if they're important to you . . .
JANE:	Yeah – I'd regret just throwing them away.
KIERAN:	You know, maybe it's because I was taught to treasure books . . . but I hate seeing students force open the pages – of paperbacks. They press so hard they end up breaking the spine.
JANE:	I know, but unfortunately, paperbacks aren't designed to last a long time and people know that. Hardbacks aren't quite as weak.
KIERAN:	Yeah, they're different, I suppose. But I still don't think people value hardbacks like they used to.
JANE:	Well, they aren't decorative, are they, like other objects. Plus, nowadays, people don't keep them out on shelves as much as they used to.
KIERAN:	That's such a pity. When I visit someone – if they have, say, a colourful book on a table, it's the first thing I'm drawn to.
JANE:	I agree – and book covers can be a work of art in themselves. Some are really eye-catching.
KIERAN:	I've always been taught to handle books carefully. If you watch someone take a book off a shelf, well, they usually do it wrong.
JANE:	Ah, my grandfather says, you should put your hand right over the top of the book . . . or if you can't do that, pull the other books on the shelf aside so that you can hold the whole cover.
KIERAN:	When did you learn all this?
JANE:	He watched me pull a heavy book off the shelf when I was small, and it fell on the floor and broke apart.
KIERAN:	Oh dear!
JANE:	I can still remember it!
KIERAN:	You know what I *really* like?
JANE:	What?
KIERAN:	The smell of new books.
JANE:	Me too.
KIERAN:	My parents used to laugh at me when I was a kid because I loved putting books up to my nose. Almost as much as reading them!
JANE:	New books aren't cheap, though, are they?
KIERAN:	I guess we're lucky we can buy them.
JANE:	My grandfather stocks second-hand books as well as new ones and they don't smell quite as good.

KIERAN:	I'd love to have a bookshop like your grandfather. What's it like?
JANE:	Well, it's quite big – it's got two floors and an attic, and he stocks all kinds of books really.
KIERAN:	I guess he treasures things like first editions and other rare books.
JANE:	Yeah – you might think he'd keep those in the attic or somewhere.
KIERAN:	. . . so they'd be hidden?

Q22

Q23

Q24

Q25

JANE:	Yeah. But he likes people to know that he has them. So, <u>he puts them out in the shop but makes sure you need a ladder to get them</u>.	Q26
KIERAN:	Right. That would prevent any thefts!	
JANE:	Uhuh.	
KIERAN:	Does he stock books for children?	
JANE:	He does. He particularly likes to encourage kids to read; he always says that he used to sit under the stairs as a child with a pile of books and read them all.	
KIERAN:	Is that where he keeps them, then?	
JANE:	Not exactly – <u>he's got a dedicated area on the ground floor with cushions so that parents can enter with their toddlers, go there and spend some time reading to them</u>.	Q27
KIERAN:	Oh cool.	
JANE:	And then there's a place for pushchairs by the front door. And a café if anyone needs refreshments.	
KIERAN:	That's good to know.	
JANE:	As I said, it's a big shop and there's a storage area out the back as well.	
KIERAN:	Oh, what does he keep there? Books he wants to throw away?	
JANE:	He hardly ever throws anything away – <u>he just leaves unwanted books by the front door for customers to take</u>.	Q28
KIERAN:	Well, that's very nice.	
JANE:	Yeah – and <u>books people or institutions have requested, they all go at the far end</u>.	Q29
KIERAN:	Oh.	
JANE:	He thinks it's best to keep these out of the main shopping area as they're boxed and new.	
KIERAN:	Did you get *your* coursebooks from him?	
JANE:	Naturally. He stocks books for a lot of the colleges. He used to keep these books on the first floor, but now there's a new university in my hometown, <u>he's moved them downstairs to attract the students. They're actually part of the coffee shop, on low shelves all around it</u>.	Q30
KIERAN:	Pretty central then. You'll have to take me there some time!	

PART 4

Tree planting now dominates political and popular agendas and is often presented as an easy answer to the climate crisis, as well as a way for business corporations to offset their carbon emissions. But unfortunately, tree planting isn't as straightforward as some people think. When the wrong trees are planted in the wrong place, it can do considerably more damage than good, failing to help either people or the environment.

Reforestation projects are currently being undertaken on a huge scale in many countries and it's crucial that the right trees are selected. A mix of species should always be planted, typical of the local natural forest ecosystem and including rare and endangered species in order to create a rich ecosystem. It's important to avoid non-native species that could become invasive. <u>Invasive species are a significant contributor to the current global biodiversity crisis and are often in competition with native species</u> and may threaten their long-term survival.   Q31

Restoring biodiversity that will maximise carbon capture is key when reforesting an area, but ideally any reforestation project should have several goals. These could include selecting trees that can contribute to wildlife conservation, <u>improve the availability of food for the local community</u> and maintain the stability of soil systems. Meeting as many of these goals as possible, whilst doing no harm to local communities, native ecosystems and vulnerable   Q32

Audioscripts

species, is the sign of a highly successful tree-planting scheme. To ensure the survival and resilience of a planted forest, it's vital to use tree seeds with appropriate levels of genetic diversity: the amount of genetic variation found within a species essential for their survival. Using seeds with low genetic diversity generally lowers the resilience of restored forests, which can make them vulnerable to disease and unable to adapt to climate change.   Q33

Choosing the right location for reforestation projects is as important as choosing the right trees. Ultimately, the best area for planting trees would be in formerly forested areas that are in poor condition. It's better to avoid non-forested landscapes such as natural grasslands, savannas or wetlands as these ecosystems already contribute greatly to capturing carbon. It would also be advantageous to choose an area where trees could provide other benefits, such as recreational spaces. Reforesting areas which are currently exploited for agriculture   Q34
should be avoided as this often leads to other areas being deforested.

Large-scale reforestation projects require careful planning. Making the right decisions about where to plant trees depends on having the right information. Having detailed and up-to-date   Q35
maps identifying high-priority areas for intervention is essential. Drone technology is a useful tool in helping to prioritise and monitor areas of degraded forest for restoration. In Brazil, it's being used to identify and quantify how parts of the Amazon are being devastated by human   Q36
activities such as rearing cattle and illegal logging.

A good example of where the right trees were picked to achieve a restored forest is in Lampang Province in Northern Thailand. A previously forested site which had been degraded through mining was reforested by a cement company together with Chiang Mai University. After spreading 60 cm of topsoil, they planted 14 different native tree species which included several species of fig. Figs are a keystone species because of the critical role they play in maintaining wildlife populations. They are central to tropical reforestation projects as they   Q37
accelerate the speed of the recovery process by attracting animals and birds which act as natural seed dispersers. This helps to promote diversity through the healthy regrowth of a wide range of plant species. Unlike the majority of fruit trees, figs bear fruit all year round, providing a reliable food source for many species. At this site, for example, after only three   Q38
rainy seasons, monkeys started visiting to eat the fig fruits, naturally dispersing seeds through defecation.

Reforestation projects should always aim to make sure that local communities are consulted and involved in the decision-making process.

The restoration of mangrove forests in Madagascar is an example of a project which has succeeded in creating real benefits for the community. Destruction of the mangrove forests   Q39
had a terrible impact on plant and animal life, and also badly affected the fishing industry, which was a major source of employment for local people living in coastal areas. The reforestation project involved hiring local people to plant and care for the new mangrove trees. Millions of mangrove trees have now been planted which has resulted in the return of a healthy aquatic ecosystem. The mangroves also act as a defence against the increased   Q40
threat of flooding caused by climate change. What's more, the local economy is more stable and thousands more Madagascans are now able to send their children to school.

One other important point to consider . . .

Listening and Reading answer keys

TEST 1

LISTENING

> Answer key with extra explanations in Resource Bank

Part 1, Questions 1–10

1. 69 / sixty-nine
2. stream
3. data
4. map
5. visitors
6. sounds
7. freedom
8. skills
9. 4.95
10. leaders

Part 2, Questions 11–20

11. B
12. A
13. B
14. C
15. A
16. G
17. C
18. B
19. D
20. A

Part 3, Questions 21–30

21&22 IN EITHER ORDER
B
D
22&24 IN EITHER ORDER
A
E
25. D
26. G
27. C
28. B
29. F
30. H

Part 4, Questions 31–40

31. walls
32. son
33. fuel
34. oxygen
35. rectangular
36. lamps
37. family
38. winter
39. soil
40. rain

If you score . . .

0–18	19–28	29–40
you are unlikely to get an acceptable score under examination conditions and we recommend that you spend a lot of time improving your English before you take IELTS.	you may get an acceptable score under examination conditions but we recommend that you think about having more practice or lessons before you take IELTS.	you are likely to get an acceptable score under examination conditions but remember that different institutions will find different scores acceptable.

Listening and Reading answer keys

TEST 1

READING

Answer key with extra explanations in Resource Bank

Reading Section 1, Questions 1–14

1. FALSE
2. FALSE
3. NOT GIVEN
4. TRUE
5. FALSE
6. NOT GIVEN
7. NOT GIVEN
8. B
9. A
10. C
11. E
12. A
13. E
14. C

Reading Section 2, Questions 15–27

15. trust
16. goals
17. strategy
18. solutions
19. pride
20. risk
21. future
22. temptations
23. completion
24. reference
25. disruption
26. failings
27. skills

Reading Section 3, Questions 28–40

28. vi
29. iii
30. viii
31. i
32. v
33. dated
34. society
35. history
36. identity
37. concepts
38. B
39. A
40. D

If you score ...

0–25	26–32	33–40
you are unlikely to get an acceptable score under examination conditions and we recommend that you spend a lot of time improving your English before you take IELTS.	you may get an acceptable score under examination conditions but we recommend that you think about having more practice or lessons before you take IELTS.	you are likely to get an acceptable score under examination conditions but remember that different institutions will find different scores acceptable.

Listening and Reading answer keys

TEST 2

LISTENING

> Answer key with extra explanations in Resource Bank

Part 1, Questions 1–10

1. Mathieson
2. beginners
3. college
4. New
5. 11 / eleven (am)
6. instrument
7. ear
8. clapping
9. recording
10. alone

Part 2, Questions 11–20

11. A
12. B
13. A
14. B
15. C
16. A
17 & 18 IN EITHER ORDER
   C
   E
19 & 20 IN EITHER ORDER
   A
   B

Part 3, Questions 21–30

21. A
22. B
23. B
24. B
25. E
26. B
27. A
28. C
29. C
30. A

Part 4, Questions 31–40

31. move
32. short
33. discs
34. oxygen
35. tube
36. temperatures
37. protein
38. space
39. seaweed
40. endangered

If you score . . .

0–20	21–29	30–40
you are unlikely to get an acceptable score under examination conditions and we recommend that you spend a lot of time improving your English before you take IELTS.	you may get an acceptable score under examination conditions but we recommend that you think about having more practice or lessons before you take IELTS.	you are likely to get an acceptable score under examination conditions but remember that different institutions will find different scores acceptable.

Listening and Reading answer keys

TEST 2

READING

Answer key with extra explanations in Resource Bank

Reading Section 1, Questions 1–14

1 D
2 A
3 C
4 E
5 C
6 B
7 B
8 TRUE
9 FALSE
10 NOT GIVEN
11 TRUE
12 FALSE
13 TRUE
14 FALSE

Reading Section 2, Questions 15–27

15 condition
16 conversation
17 hoovering
18 healthy
19 shopping
20 laundry
21 wellbeing
22 injuries
23 realistic
24 prioritise / prioritize
25 productivity
26 holiday
27 pets

Reading Section 3, Questions 28–40

28 D
29 B
30 D
31 C
32 C
33 A
34 D
35 C
36 boundaries
37 authoritative
38 permissive
39 story
40 A

If you score ...

0–25	26–32	33–40
you are unlikely to get an acceptable score under examination conditions and we recommend that you spend a lot of time improving your English before you take IELTS.	you may get an acceptable score under examination conditions but we recommend that you think about having more practice or lessons before you take IELTS.	you are likely to get an acceptable score under examination conditions but remember that different institutions will find different scores acceptable.

TEST 3

LISTENING

Answer key with extra explanations in Resource Bank

Part 1, Questions 1–10

1. harbour / harbor
2. bridge
3. 3.30 / three thirty / ½ / half 3 / three
4. Rose / rose
5. sign
6. purple
7. samphire
8. melon
9. coconut
10. strawberry

Part 2, Questions 11–20

11. C
12. D
13. F
14. G
15. B
16. H
17 & 18. *IN EITHER ORDER*
    D
    E
19 & 20. *IN EITHER ORDER*
    B
    C

Part 3, Questions 21–30

21. C
22. B
23. A
24. A
25. C
26. C
27. H
28. E
29. B
30. F

Part 4, Questions 31–40

31. clothing
32. mouths
33. salt
34. toothpaste
35. fertilisers / fertilizers
36. nutrients
37. growth
38. weight
39. acid
40. society

If you score . . .

0–17	18–27	28–40
you are unlikely to get an acceptable score under examination conditions and we recommend that you spend a lot of time improving your English before you take IELTS.	you may get an acceptable score under examination conditions but we recommend that you think about having more practice or lessons before you take IELTS.	you are likely to get an acceptable score under examination conditions but remember that different institutions will find different scores acceptable.

Listening and Reading answer keys

TEST 3

READING

Answer key with extra explanations in Resource Bank

Reading Section 1, Questions 1–14

1. E
2. C
3. A
4. B
5. D
6. A
7. B
8. D
9. B
10. C
11. A
12. C
13. C
14. A

Reading Section 2, Questions 15–27

15. list
16. reference
17. consultancy
18. outplacement
19. research
20. gaps
21. incentive
22. measurements
23. laundry allowance
24. respectable
25. hoodies
26. crutches
27. hand cuts

Reading Section 3, Questions 28–40

28. C
29. A
30. B
31. A
32. D
33. B
34. D
35. C
36. F
37. gold
38. skill
39. point
40. manuscripts

If you score ...

0–25	26–32	33–40
you are unlikely to get an acceptable score under examination conditions and we recommend that you spend a lot of time improving your English before you take IELTS.	you may get an acceptable score under examination conditions but we recommend that you think about having more practice or lessons before you take IELTS.	you are likely to get an acceptable score under examination conditions but remember that different institutions will find different scores acceptable.

Listening and Reading answer keys

TEST 4

LISTENING

> Answer key with extra explanations in Resource Bank

Part 1, Questions 1–10

1. Kaeden
2. locker(s)
3. passport
4. uniform
5. third / 3rd
6. 0412 665 903
7. yellow
8. plastic
9. ice
10. gloves

Part 2, Questions 11–20

11 & 12 *IN EITHER ORDER*
    C
    E
13 & 14 *IN EITHER ORDER*
    A
    D
15. A
16. B
17. C
18. A
19. C
20. B

Part 3, Questions 21–30

21. A
22. C
23. A
24. B
25. C
26. D
27. F
28. A
29. C
30. G

Part 4, Questions 31–40

31. competition
32. food
33. disease
34. agriculture
35. maps
36. cattle
37. speed
38. monkeys
39. fishing
40. flooding

If you score . . .

0–19	20–28	29–40
you are unlikely to get an acceptable score under examination conditions and we recommend that you spend a lot of time improving your English before you take IELTS.	you may get an acceptable score under examination conditions but we recommend that you think about having more practice or lessons before you take IELTS.	you are likely to get an acceptable score under examination conditions but remember that different institutions will find different scores acceptable.

Listening and Reading answer keys

TEST 4

READING

Answer key with extra explanations in Resource Bank

Reading Section 1, Questions 1–14

1. C
2. E
3. F
4. C
5. B
6. FALSE
7. TRUE
8. TRUE
9. FALSE
10. NOT GIVEN
11. TRUE
12. NOT GIVEN
13. FALSE
14. NOT GIVEN

Reading Section 2, Questions 15–27

15. FALSE
16. TRUE
17. FALSE
18. TRUE
19. FALSE
20. NOT GIVEN
21. NOT GIVEN
22. TRUE
23. TRUE
24. FALSE
25. 20 / twenty weeks
26. (airline) vouchers
27. (the) scholarship holder

Reading Section 3, Questions 28–40

28. maize
29. Africa
30. butterflies
31. A
32. G
33. D
34. F
35. E
36. B
37. A
38. C
39. C
40. B

If you score ...

0–26	27–33	34–40
you are unlikely to get an acceptable score under examination conditions and we recommend that you spend a lot of time improving your English before you take IELTS.	you may get an acceptable score under examination conditions but we recommend that you think about having more practice or lessons before you take IELTS.	you are likely to get an acceptable score under examination conditions but remember that different institutions will find different scores acceptable.

Sample Writing answers

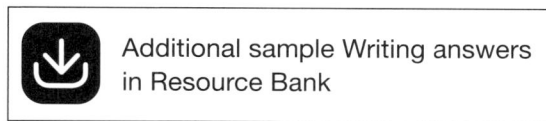

> Additional sample Writing answers in Resource Bank

TEST 1, WRITING TASK 1

This is an answer written by a candidate who achieved a **Band 6.0** score.

Dear Mr. Brent,

I hope this letter finds you well.

I am writing this letter to request my working hours in Lancom Technology to be reduced to 30 hours from 40 hours in a weekly basic.

I am requesting hours change due to study part-time. I have enrolled myself in Diploma of Logistics and Freight Forwarding. The part-time course is to be completed in 2 years time.

I would like to work from Monday to Friday from 7am to 1pm, so I could attend my classes on the afternoon session.

I hope this arrangement would allow me to gain more skills and knowledges, which I am confidently to contribute to our logistic department. Besides, the society exposure from lecturers and fellow schoolmates could contribute to our logistic network.

I am appreciate if you could look into this request and approve it. I am delighted to have face-to-face meeting with you to discuss any alternative.

Please do not hesitate to contact if you have any question. I am looking forward to hearing from you.

Thank you.

Yours sincerely.

Sample Writing answers

Here is the examiner's comment:

This letter is a good response to the task, the tone is suitable for writing to a manager and all aspects of the bullet points are presented. Benefits to the employer include [*more skills and knowledges*] that can be shared across the team, and an increased [*logistic network*]. The message can be followed as there is a clear progression, although due to the very short paragraphs, this does appear more like a list of information rather than a letter.

Vocabulary has some good elements [*enrolled | contribute to | discuss any alternative*], but there is some lack of precision in word choice [*weekly basic* / weekly schedule | *confidently to contribute* / confident will contribute]. Grammatical structures are varied but limited overall. Strengths include [*reduced to . . . from | is to be completed | so I could attend*], but there are some errors, including missing articles [*Diploma* / a Diploma] and third person 's' [*logistic network* / logistics network | *any question* / any questions], and use of modal forms [*I am appreciate* / I would appreciate | *I am delighted* / I would be delighted].

To improve the rating, the ideas should be better organised into paragraphs within the letter. Instead of starting each sentence with [*I*], the candidate could introduce more variety with linking and grammatical structures.

TEST 1, WRITING TASK 2

This is an answer written by a candidate who achieved a **Band 6.0** score.

Photography is actually be come trend. Now a day due to impact of Social Media People are not looking at the place they visit but rather concentrate on taking photographs of the place thinking that they will post them on facebook or instagram. They get a different kind of pleasure when they get more likes on their posts in the Social Media.

These are many reasons behind ??? the fact that people have access to camera and internet and social media at their fingertips they have forgotten the value of the nature of the place they are visiting.

There are negative and positive impact over this situation. Firstly when we look at good things it is good that the Technology has given an advanced accebility to the high speed internet in our pockets and high defination cameras at a cheapest price.

This helps us to capture all that we need immediately. Secondly, there is no skill or learning of a certification required for that. even a kid is able to capture beautiful pictures using Mobile Phones.

Thirdly, it is giving opportunity as not to miss any thing that we capture to share at affortable price.

Though there are positive aspects for this practices, as bad also follows good, there are negative points that we need to think about as well.

One among these is privacy, when we post some of the photographs in social media, Every one will get to know as what is happening our life. The privacy is effected.

Secondly it is giving an opportunity for fradster's to collect information like our address, Date of birth Age and so forth that they can get access to the Banking information and Scam and Rob the Money.

To conclude the positive things only give satification but the negative once are the real threat's to personal information and individuals life.

Sample Writing answers

Here is the examiner's comment:

This response covers each main area of the task: brief reasons are given on why people are taking photographs of themselves without looking at the place they are visiting (the impact of social media and the pleasure people get from the 'likes' on pictures they post) and much more detail is provided on the 'positive or negative' aspects of the trend.

There is a clear progression overall and some good cohesive features [*Firstly | Secondly | like | but*]. However, there is repetition and error [*These / There | good | privacy*] and paragraphing is not very helpful.

There is some higher-level vocabulary [*impact of | concentrate on | different kind of pleasure | get access to*] but also, some error in spelling [*accebility | high defination | affortable | fradster's | satification*] and inaccuracy [*Rob / steal | once / one*] which impacts the rating here.

Grammatical structures are mixed, with some good use [*they have forgotten the value | need to | can*], but generally, the level of error is quite high. A greater degree of accuracy in these structures would increase the score.

Overall, to achieve a higher score, the candidate should add more on 'Why do you think this is happening?' and should provide a more comprehensive conclusion. It is also important to use paragraphing more effectively, to group ideas together.

Sample Writing answers

TEST 2, WRITING TASK 1

This is an answer written by a candidate who achieved a **Band 5.0** score.

Dear Luis,

I am writing to inform you that if it is possible can you please tell the couzine to prepare some special traditional food from my country. Which is called baby corn grill for me.

This very healthy and sweet as you probably know. We are going to do a physical exercise in the club, I need to have it, because it has a huge benefit for me to against the other team. I had an experience in my country everyone must have this dish and they have done a good job, because of the digestive of the food. However, you must not eat a lot because it contains variaty of proteins. Just normal grill without any seasoning and addictives.

You should remember to let them know about that if not I will not do my best in this event. Hopefully it's ready before we start.

I look forward to hearing from you as soon as possible.

Kind regards,

Here is the examiner's comment:

This response is an attempt to address the question, but the candidate has misunderstood the requirements. The bullet points ask them to offer to make this popular dish for the club event, but this response asks the manager to arrange for the dish to be prepared. This also affects the third bullet point, where instead of explaining why the dish should be included in the International Students' club event to celebrate food, the candidate explains why their sporting team would benefit. The score for Task Achievement is affected by this inaccurate content.

Apart from the inaccurate details, there is a sense of coherence within the letter. There are linking devices [*because* | *However* | *Hopefully*] with some use of referencing [*it* | *me* | *other team* | *this*], but there are errors [*This very healthy* / It is very healthy].

Vocabulary is good enough for the task. There is some accurate use [*special traditional food* | *seasoning*] but with frequent lapses in word choice [*couzine* | *digestive of the food*] and spelling [*variaty* / variety | *addictives* / additives]. Similarly, grammatical structures are limited. There are some accurate structures, including 'if' clauses, modals, and a range of tenses [*if it is possible* | *need to have* | *have done* | *must not* | *should remember*]. However, errors do occur frequently, and punctuation is faulty and missing altogether in some places [*about that if not I will not*].

To achieve a higher score, the letter needs to fully address the task, and demonstrate a greater level of accuracy with vocabulary and grammatical structures.

Sample Writing answers

TEST 2, WRITING TASK 2

This is an answer written by a candidate who achieved a **Band 6.5** score.

Nowadays it is becoming more difficult to find the necessary time to do the home work. Even tasks as simple as cleaning the house and cooking the dinner or as important as childcare, are being delegated to third parties such as nannies or private companies.

Some people could say it is helpful to have someone who support ourselves at home. Not only because we usually do not have time to do it, but because we can promote jobs for other people. However I strongly believe that we should spend less hours at the office and much more hours at home. Doing that we should be able to carry on all the duties we use to have in the houses.

I think there certain activities we should not pass to others. For instance, taking care of our children. This is something that we, as parents, should do for ourselves. No one else could provide the kids all the love, understanding and friendship that a mother or father give to them. I remember that when I was a child, my mother quit her job and she dedicated all her time and effort to look after my brothers and I. Now, I realized that it was an invaluable time impossible to have with somebody else different from our own mother.

Summarizing, even though some people found useful to have others helping us in our duties at home, I think we should do it for ourselves because it provides valuable time at home. So that we should work less and spend more time sharing with our families. No matter if it is household chores or looking after children.

Here is the examiner's comment:

This is a strong response to the question and the candidate's position is clear from the beginning. The candidate argues that people will find most satisfaction doing the work themselves at home. There is some consideration of the other side, and the conclusion is clear and relevant.

Ideas are sequenced logically and cohesion is managed well with some good cohesive devices [*Doing that* | *Summarizing*] but some overuse. There are a few slips [*who support ourselves* / to support us]. Each paragraph presents a clear central topic.

Vocabulary is natural and accurate [*certain activities* | *quit* | *invaluable time*]. Sentence structure shows a variety of complex structures including multi-clause sentences, but a higher degree of accuracy would improve the response.

TEST 3, WRITING TASK 1

This is an answer written by a candidate who achieved a **Band 5.5** score.

Dear Mr Banks

As you know, my 6 month lease is about to expierd next month and I'm writing to you with a request to extand it for 6 more month, as my sircumstents had changed.

When I just arrived to Adelaide I was'nt sure that I'll be able to stay more then 6 month. I got a 6 month contract with my work place and that was suppuse to be it. Last week my boss who is apperoutly have a good impression of me, ask me to stay and maunage another project here in the city. So, if it's possible, I'll love to extand ower agreement. I really love the apartment, the view is lovely and the nightbrohood is friendly, although I do have one problem? The back door is broken and I'll aprishiate you help in that metter, espisialy if I'm going to stay throw the winter, which I understan can be quit cold and windy around here.

Thank you very much

Here is the examiner's comment:

This letter covers each area of the task and provides a nice level of detail. The request is to extend the lease for a further six months, plans have changed due to a work opportunity and a problem with the back door is highlighted. The tone is suitable for writing to the owner of the apartment. Ideas are organised coherently and progression is clear. There are a range of cohesive devices [So | although] and helpful use of referencing [it | who | which].

Unfortunately, there is a high level of error in spelling. This does detract from the score, which is a shame as this writer is clearly trying hard to include a good range of vocabulary. Unfortunately, the errors are noticeable because there are so many of them [expierd / expired | apperoutly / apparently | extand ower / extend our | nightbrohood / neighbourhood | espisialy / especially].

There is a mix of simple and complex grammatical structures, with some good examples [is about to | if it's possible | if I'm going to stay]. However, again, the level of error is quite high and is noticeable. There are errors in plural forms [6 more month / 6 more months] in use of past tenses [ask / asked] and future forms [I'll love to / I'd love to].

The content of this letter covers each area of the task, but to achieve a higher score, the candidate should demonstrate a greater level of accuracy with vocabulary and grammatical structures.

Sample Writing answers

TEST 3, WRITING TASK 2

This is an answer written by a candidate who achieved a **Band 5.5** score.

Yes, this is a positive trend, but when you know about that manufacturer company, about their service, quality, quantity etc. If you buy goods from you known brand then it is good for you because you get good product.

Goods are produced in local areas are cheaper than imported gods. There is a big price difference in local and imported goods. All people are not reached so those who are not afford imported goods they automatically turn to local goods.

If you buying any goods from our local brand then the money remain in our area & this is very helpful to make our economy strong. We have to buy only those product that made or produced in our area because it gives money, job to our area.

There are verious frouad companies selling duplicate of first copy imported goods. So this is also the one reason or kind of fear for not buying imported goods. There are verious charges applied when we buy imported goods and for local goods there are no such charges or taxes applied.

Hear I would like to share my experience. I buy a jeans of Lewis brand of rs 4000 after some days the colour of pant become lighter day by day, I feel very bad because I invest 4000 rs on jeans only because Lewis is an imported brand, then I thought if I buy jeans from local area then I get 4 jeans in 4000 & I realised I did mistake & from that day I choose to buy goods that are produced in my local area rather than imported goods.

I suggest you that, I you want to be a part of our developing country then buy goods from our local brands this helps to keep our money in our country.

Sample Writing answers

Here is the examiner's comment:

This response addresses both parts of the question: the reasons for consumers buying local goods, and whether this is positive or negative. In the first line, we see the writer thinks it is a positive trend. Then reasons are given for buying local goods rather than imported goods: if the product is local, it will be a good product; locally produced goods will be cheaper; the money will remain in the local area, helping the local economy with jobs and money; and buying local will avoid buying fake goods. A personal example is given to illustrate the positive trend. The conclusion is really 'giving advice' to consumers to buy local brands to develop their local economy.

There is progression through the response, but linking expressions are largely missing or incorrect [*Hear* / Here | *I suggest you that* / I suggest that]. However, cohesive devices are sometimes used well [*those who* | *our* | *those product that*] but can be faulty.

Vocabulary has an adequate range, with some good collocation, [*known brand* | *price difference* | *no such charges or taxes applied*] despite some errors in spelling [*verious frouad* / various fraud]. There are some examples of complex sentence forms, for example, in the fourth paragraph, but there are quite frequent grammatical errors.

To achieve a higher score, the candidate should present the ideas around the 'positive and negative trend' more clearly. Their conclusion should summarise the main arguments, rather than 'give advice' to local consumers. They should also demonstrate a greater level of accuracy with vocabulary and grammatical structures.

Sample Writing answers

TEST 4, WRITING TASK 1

This is an answer written by a candidate who achieved a **Band 6.0** score.

Dear Sir,

I am writing to ask for a permition about changing my position. As you know, I have already work in sales department for two years which let me learn a lot of skills of sales and helped me becoming the best sales man the season. However, I would like to require moving to Design department and I would state my reason in the following paragraphs.

First of all, I would like to thank you for giving me many chances to equip my sales skills, such as negociating with clients, promoting product and most importantly, getting over fears of meeting strangers.

However, inspite of sales skills, I eager to learn more skills in the company. Especially, I am always interest in design our company's product. Moreover, I have got some certificates from self learning and understand some design skills when I was asistanted my colleage from design department.

Besides, I really love this company. The environment and working feeling are perfect here. So, those are why I am keen to stay in this company.

Thanks you for your reading and I look forward to hearing from you soon.

Yours faithfully,

Here is the examiner's comment:

This letter is a good response to the task and the letter format is appropriate and helpful. However, the second bullet point, which is to suggest how the company would benefit, is not well covered. In the third paragraph, there is mention of an increased understanding of design skills from another department, but it is not entirely clear how this benefits the company. More could be added on this point to improve the response.

Nevertheless, ideas are arranged coherently and there is good progression. Some useful linking devices are used [*However* | *First of all* | *Moreover* | *Besides*], although they all come at the beginning of the sentence. We also have reference and substitution [*in the following paragraphs* | *are perfect here*], but there are errors [*those* / *that is*].

There is some good vocabulary, but there are also errors which detract from the score [*permition* / permission | *asistanted* / assisting] but do not have too much impact. Grammatical structures contain some stronger examples [*would like to thank you for* | *why I am keen to stay*], but overall, the level of error is quite high.

In order to score more highly, the candidate should clearly highlight all three bullet points and extend responses. There should also be greater accuracy in spelling and fewer errors in the grammatical structures.

TEST 4, WRITING TASK 2

This is an answer written by a candidate who achieved a **Band 6.5** score.

It is always a debatable topic whether photographers should follow famous people to get information about their lives. One class of people says it is good and photographers should do it while another class comments that it is not good to interferes someone's life. Before giving my opinion, I would like to discuss both the view points in detail as given in coming paragraphs.

There is one group of people who believe that photographers should always follow well known celebrities and try to get photos and information about their life. As the fans of that particular celebrity are very interested in such news and information. By getting this type of details, fans would love to follow that person's habits, style, clothing, etc. For example, one of my friend Ketul is a big fan of famous filmstar Salman Khan. He used to follow him and wearning same clothes, keeps similar hairstyle as Salman Khan is having. One more reason is that the photographers taking pictures of such famous personalities and spreading it via different social media makes that person more famous. In many cases, that celebrities like this thing.

On the other hand, another group of people believe that photographers should not do this. Following someone and taking pictures of his/her personal life is wrong. Celebrities are also a human being. They also want some space apart from their career. There are some cases where these personalities were upset and angry on photographers for doing this. For example, in December 2017, Priyanka Chopra (a famous actress) field a case against a photographer for the same.

In conclusion, I would like to say that the photographers should do this but with the permission of that celebrities. Taking pictures of someone without informing is always wrong. Getting pictures of famous personality is people's demand and famous people should always satisfy his/her fans by allowing photographers to take their pictures.

Sample Writing answers

Here is the examiner's comment:

This is a good response. The candidate presents ideas on both sides (whether it is right or wrong for photographers to follow famous people) and gives a clear opinion at the end. There is a demand for photographs of famous people; some people think it is acceptable for photographers to go ahead, as the fans demand it (an example is given of a famous film star) and some celebrities like it, as it makes them more famous; and others think it is wrong, as celebrities are also human beings who deserve some [*space*] (an example is given of another celebrity). The conclusion draws both sides together.

The response is logically organised. There are a range of linking devices [*Before | One more reason | On the other hand*] and the candidate uses cohesive devices within sentences effectively, such as referencing [*people who | that person | this type*].

Vocabulary is good with some higher-level collocation [*particular celebrity | taking pictures*]. There are a few errors in spelling [*wearning / wearing*] and word choice, but they do not impede communication. There are a variety of complex structures and frequent sentences with multiple clauses.

To achieve a higher score, the candidate should demonstrate a greater level of accuracy with vocabulary and grammatical structures.

Sample answer sheets

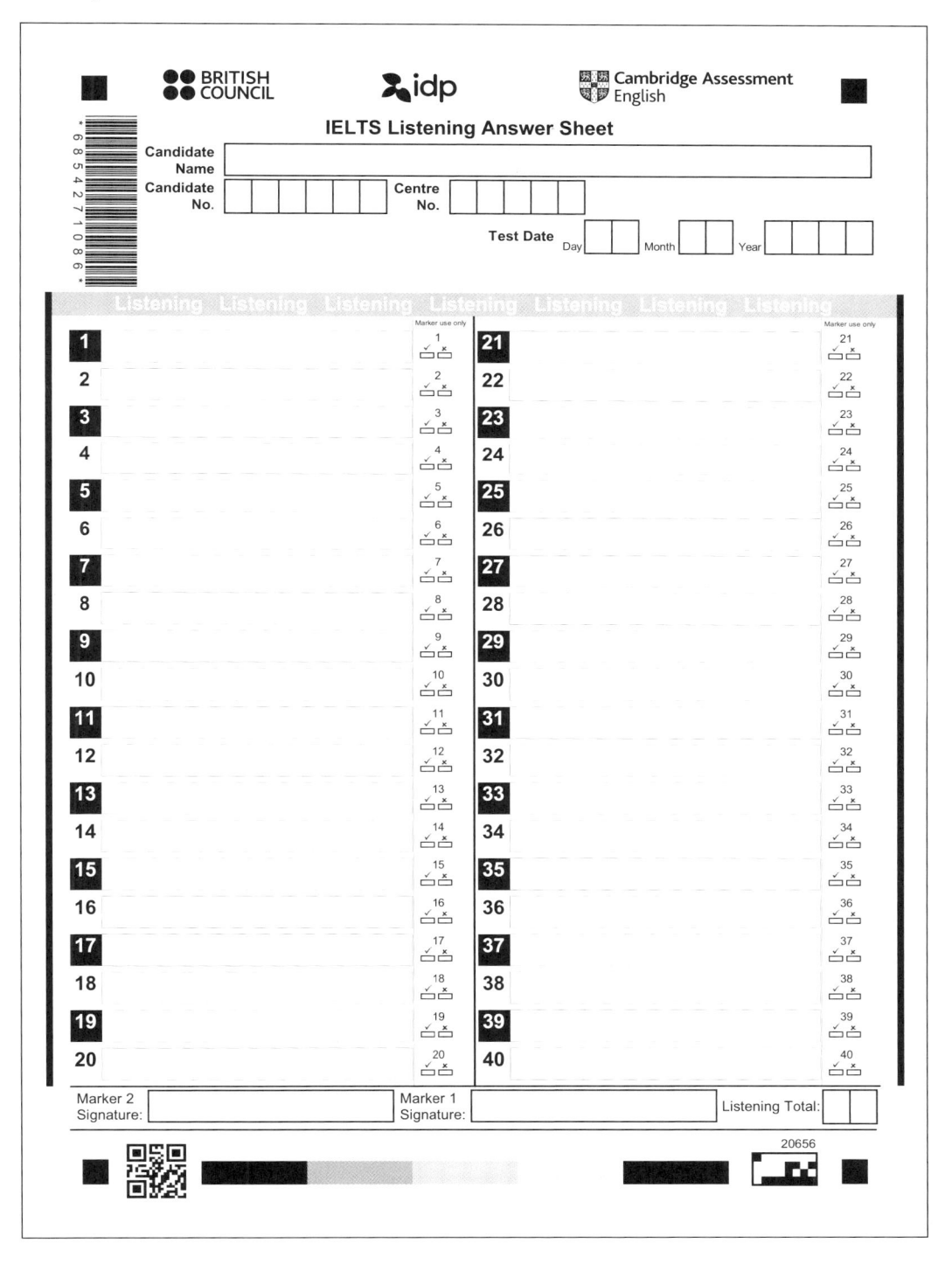

Sample answer sheets

Sample answer sheets

Sample answer sheets